FINDING
A
FOREVER HOME

FINDING
A
FOREVER HOME

True Tales from Channel 4's
The Dog House

Heather Bishop

QUERCUS

First published in Great Britain in 2022 by

QUERCUS

Quercus Editions Ltd
Carmelite House
50 Victoria Embankment
London EC4Y 0DZ

An Hachette UK company

A CIP catalogue record for this book is available
from the British Library

HB ISBN 978 1 52941 897 2
Ebook ISBN 978 1 52941 898 9

This book would not have been possible without the help and assistance
of the staff and dogs of Woodgreen Pets Charity.

Picture section: All photographs provided by the contributors.

10 9 8 7 6 5 4 3 2 1

Typeset by CC Book Production
Printed and bound in Great Britain by Clays Ltd, Elcograf S.p.A.

Papers used by Quercus Editions are from well-managed forests and other responsible sources.

CONTENTS

INTRODUCTION

In a quiet corner of the English countryside, there's a place for those looking for love. Where staff are dedicated to bringing together abandoned pets and hopeful new owners to see how lives can be changed by the perfect match.

Since it exploded onto our screens in September 2019, *The Dog House* has captured the hearts of so many viewers. We're a nation of dog lovers and seeing those magical moments as a prospective owner and dog meet for the first time and fall in love, never fails to bring a lump to the throat of even the most hardened viewer.

Described as being like *First Dates* for dogs, we go through every emotion with both hound and human as they cast eyes on each other for the very first time in the secluded meeting pen. Will it be love at first sight or will they both be bolting for the door?

The show is filmed at Woodgreen Pets Charity in Cambridgeshire that takes in hundreds of disowned or neglected dogs, cats, and other small pets every year, as well as pups whose owners can't look after them any more due to a variety of reasons such as illness or a change in circumstances. Cameras follow the work of dedicated staff members who are committed to matching abandoned dogs with loving new owners. For many animals, Woodgreen is their last chance at a happy life. Every year, the charity helps some of the most unloved and unwanted pets to get back on their paws and find them a new forever home, as well as offering help and support to pet owners across the country

In an average year, they rehome around seven hundred dogs aided by three hundred dedicated members of staff and seven hundred volunteers. There are more owners than ever willing to give a dog a second chance at happiness. Enquiries to Woodgreen more than trebled during the pandemic with twenty thousand people contacting the centre about getting a pet between April and June 2020. The average length of a stay for most dogs at Woodgreen is thirty to thirty-five days but this can vary because the charity works with a number of dogs that have complex medical and behavioural needs. The longest ever stay was for a dog called Whitefield who was at Woodgreen for a record five hundred and thirty-five days before finding a new home.

*

But what happens when the cameras stop rolling? Is it happy ever after for our doggy friends and will their new owners have found what they were looking for in their rescue pets?

Here you can read some of the most heart-breaking and inspirational stories of the participants who came to *The Dog House* searching for their forever furry friend and hear how rehoming a rescue dog has changed their lives.

Find out more about the members of staff too. The familiar faces at Woodgreen who help the participants week after week also have emotional stories of their own to share.

Welcome to *The Dog House*.

For more information about Woodgreen Pets Charity
go to woodgreen.org.uk

CHAPTER ONE

Midnight

They held hands and stared at the screen, waiting excitedly to see the first glimpse of their baby. The sonographer who was doing their twelve-week scan suddenly paused.

'I'm just going to get someone else to have a look at this,' she told them.

It was the hesitant tone of her voice that made Joanne and Tony Wharam instinctively know that there was something seriously wrong.

All Joanne had ever wanted to be in life was a mum. She and Tony were twenty-one and had just moved into their first flat together, and although this pregnancy hadn't been planned, it was a happy surprise. Once they'd got over the shock, they'd spent the past few weeks getting excited, discussing baby names and making plans for their new life as a family of three.

But now, in a matter of minutes, all their hopes and dreams were shattered. The doctor told them that it was a missed miscarriage. This is where the fetus dies or stops developing but stays in the womb so there's no indication of a problem.

It was devastating but it made them determined to try for another baby as soon as possible. However, every month led to crushing disappointment as they failed to get pregnant again. When months turned into years, they went to see their GP. Tests didn't find anything wrong with either of them and frustratingly it was put down to 'unexplained infertility'.

After five years of trying and failing to conceive, they turned to IVF. They were eligible for treatment on the NHS so they decided to start immediately after their wedding in 2016.

'It's going to work first time,' smiled Tony, as they lay by the pool on their honeymoon in Turkey.

Joanne felt the same. She'd got pregnant once so she was convinced IVF was the answer to their problems.

Filled with hope and excitement, they couldn't wait to get started and finally have their much-longed-for baby.

The treatment went well and they ended up with three embryos – one of which was implanted. They then had to wait two weeks before they could do a pregnancy test to see if it had worked. Joanne did everything the doctors had advised to give this embryo the best possible chance. She took two weeks off work to rest and try to relax and fill her mind with positive thoughts.

She'd coped well with the medical side of IVF but this part felt like psychological torture. The wait was excruciating and she spent her time over-analyzing every little sign, wondering if each was an indication that she was pregnant.

Finally the day came at last and Joanne got up early to do a pregnancy test. She and Tony paced the bedroom, nervously waiting for the result to show up on the plastic stick.

It was negative.

Naively perhaps, they'd both been convinced that it was going to work first time and they were devastated.

Joanne sat on the bed in her dressing gown and sobbed.

'It's all my fault,' she cried.

Why couldn't her body be normal and do what it was biologically designed to do?

Tony was silent, desperately trying to stay strong for Joanne. He hated seeing her get so upset and blaming herself. All they could do was stay positive and try again as soon as possible with the remaining two embryos. NHS regulations stipulated they had to wait three months between cycles so the next few weeks were a countdown to when they could start trying again. But there was more devastation when their second cycle failed too.

Again, they picked themselves up and moved as quickly as they could onto their third and final attempt. Everything went well and they were on their way to the hospital for the embryo to be implanted when Joanne's mobile rang. It was a nurse from the IVF clinic.

'I'm so sorry,' she told her. 'The embryo didn't survive the thawing process.'

With nothing to implant, their IVF journey and their last chance of having a biological child of their own was over. The thought of never being a family, of never experiencing that feeling of holding their baby in their arms was unbearable. Joanne cried and cried but Tony didn't say a word.

The crushing disappointment each time the IVF had failed had got harder and harder to bear and Tony was struggling to cope.

They both handled their grief differently. Joanne reached out to friends and family for support, but Tony bottled things up.

He wouldn't talk to her and started drinking every night. The more she worried about him, the further he seemed to push her away and she felt helpless. It was hard to see the person she was married to in such a bad way and not feel able to help him.

There was obviously something seriously wrong and she was worried that it was her. Now that she wasn't able to have a baby, did he not love her any more?

He came in from work one evening and didn't say a word to her.

'Please talk to me Tony and tell me what's wrong,' she begged him.

'Just leave me alone, I'm going for a drive.'

He knew he was being a horrible person to be around but he was angry with himself and with the world.

As he sped down twisting country lanes, dark thoughts ran through Tony's head.

If I crash now then I won't have to deal with all of this pain and hurt any more, he thought to himself.

When he got home, he started drinking heavily. After too many cans of lager, he broke down and finally opened up to Joanne.

'I'm not coping,' he cried.

Joanne was shocked as she hadn't realized how much he'd been struggling. Endless years of trying for a baby and being on the constant treadmill of fertility treatment had pushed Tony to the edge. He was clearly depressed and she knew their marriage would never survive if things carried on like this. So she made a decision. She desperately wanted a baby and they had talked about trying more IVF privately, but not at the cost of everything else. For the sake of their marriage and Tony's mental health, she knew they needed to stop.

'Let's forget about IVF and get on with our lives,' she told him.

'Are you sure?' he asked her.

Joanne nodded. 'I don't want to lose you too,' she said.

Tony eventually went to the doctor and was put on antidepressants and slowly his mental health started to improve.

It was a relief for both of them to live their lives again and not worry any more. They had nights out and went on holiday. They now realized that IVF had completely taken over. They hadn't been able to plan anything as everything had been centered around their next cycle of treatment.

Yet their determination to be parents was still there so, a year after their last failed IVF, Joanne made an appointment with an adoption agency to find out more about what the process would involve.

When she told Tony someone from the agency was going to come and talk to them at home, she could see there was something on his mind.

'What is it?' she asked, concerned that he had started to worry about the adoption process.

'Shall we try one more round of IVF?' he suggested.

He was in a good place with his mental health and he knew that both he and Joanne weren't quite ready to give up on the dream of having a biological child of their own yet.

'Only if you're really sure that you're OK with it,' she told him.

They would have to fund it privately this time so they took loans out on credit cards to pay for it.

Again they had three viable embryos and two were

implanted during the first cycle to maximize their chances. Joanne was filled with hope. Surely this time it had to work?

Sadly it didn't and they both felt that familiar sense of devastation and loss as they stared at a negative pregnancy test. They quickly reverted back to their familiar patterns.

Tony was a plumber and had to go to work that day, so he buried his grief and carried on like nothing had happened. Joanne, who found it impossible to put on a brave face, stayed at home and sobbed.

Even though they had one embryo left, mentally they prepared themselves for the worst. Every other attempt had failed so why would this time be any different? After nearly a decade of trying for a baby, they were both done with the endless disappointment.

'Let's get a dog,' Joanne suggested.

Tony's face lit up at the thought and she hadn't seen him that happy in months.

She was desperate to have someone or something that needed them and was dependent on them so they could experience that feeling of unconditional love. They both had so much love to give and if they couldn't give it to a baby then why not to a dog instead?

Perhaps a dog would make them feel like a proper family and help take away that constant gnawing feeling that something was missing in their lives.

They'd both had dogs growing up and Tony had been

especially close to his – a rescue mongrel called Bonnie. Every morning as a child, he'd get up early so he could go downstairs and sleep on the sofa with her and he wanted to experience that special bond again. Bonnie had come from Woodgreen which wasn't far from their home in Lincolnshire so that's who they contacted.

Their story struck a chord with pet advisor Helen who'd also struggled to get pregnant with her first baby. Her dogs had helped her through that difficult time and she remembered what a difference it had felt to have someone in her life who loved her no matter what.

The couple wanted a cuddly dog that they could nurture and who would give them that absolute love and affection that they craved. But when it came to breeds, they had different tastes. Joanne wanted a smaller dog like a Cockapoo, whereas Tony wanted something a bit bigger and more masculine.

The team struggled at first but eventually they came up with one option. Midnight was a Patterjack – a Patterdale terrier crossed with a Jack Russell – who'd been brought in with two other terriers. Their owner was a hoarder and life at the house had been chaotic. Midnight was quite a nervous and timid dog but once he got to know people, he loved his cuddles.

As soon as he was brought into the meeting pen, Tony and Joanne were smitten by this cute black-haired seven-month-old puppy.

'Oh my God,' they gasped.

For Tony, it was love at first sight. He couldn't believe it when Midnight went straight over to him, jumped up and covered him in licks. The pair seemed to have an instant connection; however, Joanne was more hesitant. Midnight didn't seem that interested in her and she was worried that they wouldn't have the same attachment.

Sensing her fears, the staff arranged for her to spend time on her own with him in the meeting pen. He took a few treats from her but even then, he ran to the door and she was nervous that he didn't want to be alone with her.

Afterwards they took Midnight for a walk around the grounds at Woodgreen. As Tony took his lead, he smiled as the terrier insisted on sniffing around every patch of grass. They'd only just met this dog but Joanne could already see an instant change in her husband.

She couldn't remember the last time she'd seen him so happy and they both agreed they wanted to adopt him.

However, the one thing that had struck them both was that Midnight's name didn't really suit him. He was a cute, scrappy little pup whereas Midnight, although it was a great name, sounded like it should belong to a bigger, more menacing dog.

'What are we going to call you, my little buddy?' asked Tony as they walked along.

Joanne laughed.

'There you go – I think you've just found his new name,' she smiled.

They were worried it would take him time to adjust but he answered to it straight away.

It was a month before they could bring Buddy home to Stamford. They couldn't wait to have him with them full time, although Joanne was still nervous that he wouldn't attach to her like he had instantly done to Tony. Staff at Woodgreen had also warned them he might be a bit timid at first and take a while to settle in.

However, the minute they opened the front door of the house, Buddy shot in. They both laughed as he sprinted round and round each room at lightning speed, then he jumped onto the sofa and curled up.

It was as if he knew he was home and he settled straight away.

Joanne was still unsure how he was going to be with her because all he'd seemed to want at Woodgreen was to be with Tony. She was anxious that he wasn't going to bond with her at all. That night they sat on the sofa watching TV when a little black figure appeared by her feet and a pair of big brown eyes stared up at her. Joanne automatically assumed that he'd go to Tony. But much to her surprise, Buddy jumped up onto the sofa, climbed into her lap and curled up. Feeling this little warm body snuggled against her, Joanne felt that pull of complete love that she'd been desperate to feel for so long. This little thing was dependent on them and it felt wonderful.

While he reserved his licks for Tony, he saved his cuddles for her and he bonded with them both. The only thing he didn't take to was the dog bed they'd bought for him. While his new bed lay empty downstairs, Buddy preferred to snuggle up at the bottom of their bed, burying himself in the duvet by their feet.

A couple of weeks after Buddy arrived, they started their last round of IVF. It was their one remaining embryo and they both knew this was their final chance at having a biological child of their own. They knew after this they couldn't carry on – emotionally and financially.

This time, Tony approached it differently. For him, because they'd got Buddy it felt like the pressure was off. If it didn't work then he knew they still had someone to love and care for who loved them back.

He still had his down days and there were times that he couldn't stop the dark thoughts from creeping in. He knew how much this meant to Joanne and how desperate she was to be a mum. He couldn't bear to think of how disappointed she was going to be if it failed again.

It was like Buddy had a sixth sense and knew when Tony needed some extra love. Tony was sat watching TV one night, his heart heavy with worry, when Buddy came over to him and lay on his chest. The way Buddy cuddled up to him reminded Tony of his childhood dog Bonnie. Buddy instinctively knew what his dad needed and he instantly calmed and reassured him.

Tony didn't feel overwhelmed like he had when they'd done IVF in the past. After a long day of working alone, as he drove home he felt that familiar sinking feeling in his stomach. But as soon as the front door opened, a little furry face appeared and he was covered in licks and his mood instantly changed. He couldn't feel down for long with Buddy around, who cheered him up as soon as he walked in the house.

Joanne could see the change in him too. When they'd gone through previous IVFs, Tony would get in from work and she could tell he was low. He wouldn't want to talk to her or even eat. But this time, he was so excited to see Buddy and Buddy jumped up and down, Tony would jump up and down with him. He'd take him for long walks to clear his head and she could see his mood had lifted and he was a lot happier. She could tell straight away that he was back to the old Tony and it felt like a weight had lifted for her too.

This round of IVF also felt different for her. If she was being honest, mentally she'd already given up. The past four attempts hadn't worked so why should this round be any different? Ever since their first round of IVF when she had stayed at home for the dreaded two-week wait until test day, she had continued to work during that fortnight. This time, because they'd just got Buddy, she decided to take the time off work so she could spend it with him. He was the perfect distraction. He was a little ball of energy so she took him for walks and then they'd curl up together on the sofa. She found it a lot easier to chill out with Buddy snuggled in her lap, wanting a stroke.

One morning, towards the end of the two weeks, she woke up as normal and waved Tony off to work. She was still in her dressing gown, padding around in the kitchen with Buddy, when she suddenly decided to take a pregnancy test.

She was still a few days off the official two-week wait and she knew it might even be too early to get a result but something told her to do it. Every other time she'd done one Tony had been with her, but this time she didn't want him to experience that same disappointment. She was still convinced it wasn't going to work so why put him through that emotional turmoil again?

Joanne wanted to get it out of the way as quickly as possible and move on with their lives. She did the test and sat on the bed with Buddy.

She tried not to, but she kept glancing over at the plastic stick on the bedside table.

'It's OK, Buddy,' she sighed, almost trying to reassure herself. 'Whatever happens we've got you.'

A few minutes later, she glanced at it again. She stared at the screen and did a double take.

Surely it was a mistake or she'd read it wrong?

Then she looked again, hardly daring to believe what the test was telling her.

She was pregnant.

After nearly ten years of trying, five attempts at IVF, endless heartache and lots of tears, they'd finally done it.

It didn't seem real. In fact, all morning Joanne kept checking the test to make sure the result hadn't changed but the words on the screen remained the same.

She was desperate to tell Tony but she didn't want to ring him at work and break the news to him over the phone so she came up with a plan.

As she heard his car pull up in the driveway that night, she put Buddy into the kitchen. She knew the first thing Tony would do was run to the dog but tonight she wanted his full attention.

Sure enough, the first thing he asked when he walked in was: 'Where's the dog?'

'He's in the kitchen because I've got something really important to show you and I didn't want him to distract you,' she told him.

She led him into the living room where there was a little stuffed elephant, a card with a rainbow on the front and six words spelt out in scrabble letters.

You're going to be a daddy.

Tony looked at the display laid out in front of him and looked at Joanne, confused.

She handed him the pregnancy test and saw the look of surprise on his face as he read what was on it.

'You're joking?' he gasped.

She shook her head.

'No I'm not,' she grinned. 'You're going to be a daddy.'

Neither of them could believe that after all these years it was really happening. Their friends and family were so excited for them.

'It's because you've got Buddy,' Tony's mum told them. 'That's why the IVF worked this time.'

Part of them couldn't help but think she was right. They'd thought they were rescuing him but the reality was, he'd rescued them and picked them up when they were at their lowest point.

As her pregnancy progressed, Joanne was anxious the whole time. After everything that had happened, she knew she wouldn't truly relax until she had a healthy baby in her arms.

As a sales assistant, she was on her feet on the shop floor all day so halfway through her pregnancy she went down to part-time hours. She spent those days at home, relaxing on the sofa with Buddy.

He'd always been a bouncy, excitable dog but as her bump grew, he instinctively knew he had to be gentle around her. He didn't jump up at her any more and instead of lying on her lap like he always did, he carefully positioned himself under her bump like a protective cushion.

In April 2020, Joanne went into labour and baby Willow was born by emergency C-section. After all the years of trying and hoping, Joanne couldn't believe that she was finally a mum and she couldn't stop staring at her beautiful daughter. It was the same for Tony. It felt like the gloom had lifted and they could enjoy their lives as a family.

Three days later, Tony and Joanne were finally able to bring their much-longed-for daughter home to meet Buddy.

They were both anxious about introducing him to Willow. The one thing they'd worried about was how he was going to feel when the baby arrived. Ever since they'd got him from Woodgreen, he'd been the centre of their world and they didn't want him to feel like he'd been pushed out.

At the back of their minds, they couldn't help but worry about what would happen if he reacted badly to the baby. Tony's sister had looked after Buddy overnight while they were at the hospital and Tony went and picked him up when he came home. They wanted to make sure Buddy was already in the house when they brought Willow in rather than the other way round.

Filled with nerves, Joanne carried Willow through the front door. He was such an excitable dog, and they were worried that he would jump up. Tony got down on the floor with Buddy and kept him close as Joanne brought Willow into the room.

'Hey Buddy, this is your sister Willow,' she told him gently, putting the car seat down on the floor.

Keeping a firm hold of his collar, Tony slowly led him over to her. They both watched anxiously as Buddy edged curiously over to Willow. He bent down and gently gave her head a quick sniff, then he ran over to his favourite spot on the sofa and curled up, disinterested in the new arrival.

Despite all their worries, Buddy turned out to be the softest, most gentle dog. Whenever Willow cried, he ran over to her to check that she was OK and gave her head a gentle sniff or a lick. He never jumped up when either of them had her in their arms.

As Willow grew older, she was obsessed with Buddy. Her eyes followed him wherever he went and when he had his mad moments of sprinting around the house she would giggle and shriek. She would reach out and grab his collar or his fur, but he would never flinch.

One morning, when Willow was a year old, Joanne went to get her from her cot. As usual, as soon as she opened the stairgate in Willow's bedroom doorway, Buddy rushed in.

Willow had already pulled herself up to standing and was jumping about because there was only one person she wanted to see. Buddy ran over to her and stuck his nose through the cot bars and gave her a gentle lick.

'Doggy!' she yelled excitedly. 'Doggy!'

It was one of her first words and Joanne couldn't believe it.

Afterwards Joanne brought Willow into their bed to give her her morning milk while Buddy lay at their feet, snuggled under the duvet with them.

Relaxing at home one afternoon on the sofa, Tony looked

across at Joanne. Willow had nodded off on her chest and Buddy was curled up on his lap fast asleep. It was at that moment, he suddenly realized that he had everything that he'd ever wanted. They'd been trying to have a baby for nearly ten years and it had caused so much stress and disappointment. Suddenly it felt like the dark days were behind them and they could finally enjoy life as a family.

Buddy had arrived when they had needed him the most and he'd brought them so much joy and comfort. He'd made them feel like the family they'd feared they'd never be, and healed the hole in their hearts. Now, with their beloved Willow too, they finally felt complete.

CHAPTER TWO

Norman

Lorraine Pendlington knocked gently on the bedroom door, hoping to coax her son, Oliver, to come out.

'Come on, Oliver,' she told him gently. 'Let's go out for a walk. You could do with the fresh air.'

'No thank you,' he said firmly. 'I'd rather stay in my room. I want to be at home.'

Lorraine's heart sank and she was so worried about him.

Lorraine had three sons – James, Will and Oliver, who, at twenty-five, was her youngest. They had been a close family since Lorraine's husband Matthew had died very suddenly from a heart attack at the age of fifty, leaving her as a single parent to the boys. Lorraine had been the main breadwinner and she'd been out at work every day as a product developer for lingerie and swimwear, while Matthew had looked after the boys. He'd been incredibly close to all of them and especially to Oliver who had only been twelve when he died.

Oliver had high-functioning autism and they had known he was different from an early age. He was non-verbal and he wouldn't eat or make eye contact with people. Matthew had fought hard for his son and he'd been diagnosed at the age of three.

Since then, Oliver had come such a long way. He was highly intelligent and had recently finished a master's degree in Film Studies at Sussex University. He was very good at expressing himself and loved running and volunteering.

He suffered from anxiety, which meant he would struggle to live independently, but Lorraine and his brothers were so proud of all that he'd achieved.

When the UK went into a national lockdown due to Covid in March 2020, Oliver's life drastically changed overnight. He was someone who thrived on structure and routine and before lockdown, his days had been full. Three mornings a week he studied at the library and the other two he volunteered at the Amnesty International shop. He was a member of the local running club and he went to the cinema at least twice a week. Lorraine knew Oliver thrived on being busy and having a purpose.

Then the first lockdown happened. Much to Lorraine's relief, Oliver had been OK at first. The rules were strict but

Oliver knew what they could or couldn't do and he liked that rigidity.

Lorraine created their own routine at home. Every morning they'd each do a Joe Wicks workout, then they'd go out for a walk for their daily allotted hour of exercise. In the afternoons and evenings they'd either watch a film together or do a Zoom call with his brothers. Oliver was anxious about the virus and what was going to happen to the world but, in a bid to make him feel more secure, Lorraine made sure that he had order and structure and knew what was going to happen each day.

But once Covid restrictions had started to ease and change a few months later, Lorraine could see that Oliver was struggling to cope and that his anxiety had increased.

He would no longer come out for their daily walk, which really worried Lorraine. They lived in Hove and they were allowed back on the beaches. Lorraine was desperate to go for a swim in the sea and meet other people for a walk now they were allowed to but Oliver wouldn't even entertain it.

She could tell that he was fearful of going outside and was becoming a bit of a hermit. He had so much time on his hands and he was constantly reading every single bit of news and obsessing about it. He was scared something was going to happen to him or Lorraine and she could see that it was all getting too much for him.

Lorraine went and sat with Oliver in his bedroom and he admitted that he was struggling.

'Mum I'm scared,' he told her tearfully. 'I don't want to go out and I don't want you to go out either. I don't want you to die.'

She could see how frightened he was and she did her best to reassure him.

'Look we'll go out really early in the morning when there will hardly be anybody around and then we'll stay at home for the rest of the day,' she told him.

So that's what they did.

Lorraine came up with new ways to distract Oliver from the fear and the worry of the news. She taught him how to do some basic cooking, they did housework together and she encouraged him to do some Zoom yoga sessions.

But every time the rules changed, Oliver struggled, and she could see how overwhelming it was for him. He started to get very depressed and the sense of isolation and uncertainty was sending his anxiety levels through the roof.

She spoke to Will, James and James' partner, Eve, about it.

'I'm so worried about Ollie,' she told them. 'He's getting very stressed and he's very upset and tearful and his anxiety has ramped right up.'

They were concerned too.

Oliver had always suffered from anxiety but before the pandemic, Lorraine could tell when he was getting stressed and had strategies that she'd use to deflect and distract him. She'd book cinema tickets or they'd go and visit a friend.

But now, because of lockdown, they couldn't do any of those things.

'Mum why don't you get another rescue dog?' suggested Will. 'But this time one that gets on with Oliver.'

'I think that's a great idea,' she agreed.

A dog might encourage Oliver to leave the house and Lorraine thought it would be good for him to feel a sense of responsibility for something other than himself. It might help lower his anxiety levels too.

Oliver struggled to make friends and having a dog who gave him unconditional love was something that she thought would really benefit him.

However, Lorraine also knew it wasn't going to be easy to find the right dog. Their rescue dog – a Patterdale terrier called Louis – had died the previous year. He was a crotchety old thing who, as he'd got older, had reacted badly to Oliver. Louis would growl at him and he wouldn't let Oliver pet him. He marked his territory by weeing in Oliver's bedroom and he barked a lot – unexpectedly and suddenly – which was stressful and upsetting for Oliver. It had got to the point where Lorraine couldn't even have visitors at the house because Louis was so grumpy.

Last year Louis had died of old age. She hadn't intended on getting another dog because Oliver was studying and she was busy working.

But now that Covid had grounded them both, Lorraine was

convinced that getting another rescue dog would really help Oliver. She knew they would have to be carefully matched: Oliver's autism meant that he sometimes made sudden, rapid movements. Out of the blue, he would flap his arms and make noises, and those who didn't know him couldn't be sure if he was anxious or happy. Over the years, Oliver had learnt coping strategies so he didn't react like that in certain social situations. It rarely happened at university or when he was volunteering but Lorraine knew what an effort it was for him to control it. At home, it happened a lot and she wanted him to be able to relax and truly be himself in his own house and not worry about controlling his behaviour. But she also knew that some dogs would react badly to these sudden noises and movements. Louis had hated it and other dogs they'd come across over the years had been panicked by it too.

'Before I talk to Oliver, I want to look at some of the rescues a bit more,' Lorraine told Will, James and Eve.

There was one place at the top of her list. For a while, she'd been following Woodgreen on Instagram and she'd been really impressed with the care they took to match the dogs with their new owners. She felt they could be the answer for what would have to be a sensitive match.

One evening she had a chat to Oliver.

'I think it would be a really good idea for us to get another dog,' she told him. 'I think it would be great for you to have a buddy.'

He was keen but she could see the worry on his face.

'I want to, but what if we get one and it doesn't like me?' he sighed.

Lorraine understood his fears and she shared them too. Hoping to reassure him, she showed him Woodgreen's Instagram account.

'I was thinking about contacting this place,' she told him.

She explained that Woodgreen were determined to pair people up with the right dog and spent a lot of time discussing what sort of dog would suit you.

'But what if it's like Louis?' Oliver worried.

'All rescue dogs are different,' Lorraine reassured him. 'Look at Tyke.'

Tyke was James and Eve's rescue dog. He was super nervous around people but even when Oliver was making his noises, Tyke would just sit calmly at his feet.

Lorraine knew it was going to be hard as there were no guarantees of how any dog would react to someone with autism. There were some dogs who just wouldn't be able to handle Oliver's brain pattern and would be stressed out. It was so dependent on their personality. They were like people; some were just more understanding than others. It needed to be a perfectly balanced match and she felt a responsibility to her son to get it right.

The following day, Lorraine contacted Woodgreen. As the country was still in the middle of lockdown, the rescue home could take people's details but they couldn't place any dogs at that point. Excitingly a few weeks later they emailed to see if she would be interested in having a chat with someone from *The Dog House.* Lorraine knew it was going to be a difficult search so she jumped at the chance of having some extra help from the TV show.

In July 2020, they drove the three hours to Woodgreen. Lorraine was still so nervous that they would get it wrong. Her big fear was that they'd be matched with a dog that didn't work out, and then they'd have to give it back. The thought was so unbearable that she'd already decided that if that happened, James would take the dog.

'I'm scared that it won't like me,' Oliver admitted in the car on the way there.

'It will be OK,' she reassured him. 'We're going to find a great dog that understands and accepts you.'

She hoped that she was right.

Lorraine was reassured as soon as they got to Woodgreen. Pet advisor Helen spent a long time talking to Oliver, working out what he wanted, and Oliver was very open about his fears.

'I've got high-functioning autism and sometimes dogs react badly to that,' he told her.

Lorraine explained that for them, personality rather than breed was key.

Oliver wanted a friendly dog who he had an instant rapport with.

Because they'd mentioned that they liked the personalities of Staffordshire bull terriers, Helen's first suggestion was Cynthia – a two-year-old Staffie cross. She was tactile, affectionate and friendly – everything Lorraine and Oliver said they were looking for in a dog.

She'd come to Woodgreen as a stray and was a little bit nervous when she first met people but she loved cuddles.

Waiting in the meeting pen, Lorraine was excited to meet her but she was also very nervous.

She knew they would instinctively feel if a dog was right for them or not. Her view was that a dog either liked you or it didn't – there was no halfway house. A bond could grow but she felt they'd know instantly if it was going to work.

Cynthia was gorgeous but as soon as she was brought into the meeting pen, Lorraine could tell she was very nervous. When her handler left, she scratched at the door and howled to get out.

Lorraine and Oliver sat patiently on the floor and waited for her to approach them. When she finally came over, they gave her some treats. Oliver was delighted when she sat and offered him her paw in return.

'Good girl,' he smiled.

But Lorraine was having reservations. Cynthia was a lovely dog but Lorraine could tell that she wasn't interested in getting to know them. She wanted to get out of that pen and leave. When Oliver started making some of his noises, she looked terrified and that was all the confirmation Lorraine needed. Sadly it wasn't going to work. By now, Oliver felt the same.

'I don't think she's going to bond with us Mum, is she?' he sighed.

When Helen came into the meeting pen, Lorraine told her what they were thinking.

'It doesn't feel right,' she sighed. 'I'm afraid we're not feeling the connection and I don't think Cynthia is either.'

Luckily Helen had another dog in mind. Norman was a sweet West Highland terrier who'd recently been found abandoned at the side of a country road. His fur was badly matted and he was underweight, and staff suspected that he'd been sleeping rough for several weeks. He wasn't microchipped and no one had come to claim him.

'Even after everything he's been through, he's such a happy little chappy,' Helen told them. 'He's very friendly, sociable and outgoing, and very active.'

They thought he was around nine years old.

When Norman waddled into the meeting pen on his little Westie legs, Lorraine couldn't help but smile. He had such a cute face and one ear that flopped down over his eyes. Again, they tried not to rush or overwhelm him. They sat patiently on the floor while he sniffed his way inquisitively around the meeting pen.

Eventually he came over to them and Oliver fed him some treats and Lorraine gave him a stroke.

'Let's see if he plays,' said Oliver, picking up the ball.

As soon as he threw it, Norman immediately chased after it, wagging his tail excitedly.

Lorraine could see how happy Oliver was as he ran round throwing the ball to him.

'I think you've got yourself a friend there,' she smiled.

It was clear to her that Oliver felt an immediate connection to this dog.

'There's something quite special about Norman,' Oliver agreed.

Lorraine could see that he was a chilled-out dog and he wasn't nervous around them at all – and he seemed to like them too. The staff had told her that he didn't like being held but he let her pick him up and put him on the bench.

They went for a walk and Lorraine looked at Oliver as he took Norman's lead. She could see that Norman had the same effect on Oliver as running did. When Lorraine watched Oliver run, it was as if she could see the stresses and strains of the world disappear behind him. And it was the same when he was with Norman. As he walked along holding his lead, Oliver was relaxed, smiling and chatty. She could see it felt so natural to him.

'What do you think then?' she asked.

'Oh yes please can we take him?' Oliver immediately replied.

She could see how taken he was with him, and if Oliver was happy, Lorraine was too.

'I think he's going to be a really special dog for you,' she told him. 'You're going to be good buddies.'

They had to wait four weeks before they could collect Norman. He'd had an operation to remove some cancerous lumps from his neck and he needed to be monitored for a little bit longer to check that he'd recovered and was putting on weight.

In September 2020, Lorraine went back to Woodgreen to pick Norman up. Unfortunately, Oliver was ill and had to stay at home so she went with James. It was a three-hour journey back from Woodgreen to their home in Hove and Lorraine was worried about how Norman was going to cope. Their previous rescue dog Louis was terrified of going in the car and had howled the entire way home when they'd first collected him. In a way, Lorraine was pleased Oliver wasn't with them because if Norman did get upset, she knew that it would really stress him out.

James had a van and as Lorraine put Norman gently into the doggy car seat next to her in the front, he didn't bat an eyelid. He was very inquisitive and seemed quite happy sat there for the entire journey, watching the world go by out of the window while Lorraine fed him bits of boiled chicken.

She knew Oliver was so excited to see him and he was sat there waiting when they got home. As Norman wobbled into the house on his stubby legs, he instantly made himself at home.

The vet at Woodgreen had picked up that he'd got arthritis in his back legs and had some mobility issues, and they'd decided to put his bed downstairs in the kitchen so he didn't have to worry about getting up and down the stairs.

'I think we've got to be prepared for an unsettled week,' Lorraine had pre-warned Oliver.

Norman was in another strange place and she expected it would take time for him to settle at night. They'd both agreed to take it in turns to sleep downstairs with him so they could make sure he was OK. Lorraine knew that was a big deal for Oliver because it was a change from his usual routine.

Lorraine slept downstairs with Norman for the first couple of nights and, much to her surprise, Norman was absolutely fine. He was warm and cosy in his bed and he settled straight in so there was no need for Oliver to take his turn.

As soon as Norman arrived, Oliver's life changed. He had a focus for his day and the structure and order again that he liked.

All of a sudden he had a purpose again. The day after Norman arrived, Lorraine heard noises downstairs at 6.30 a.m. She went down to find Oliver up and dressed.

'I'm taking Norman for a walk,' he told her.

He was out of the door by 6.40 a.m.

When he got back an hour later, she could see Oliver was relaxed and ready to face the day.

'I'm going to get him his breakfast now,' he smiled.

Before Norman had arrived, Oliver had still got up very early but after he'd had breakfast he was aimless and struggled to know what to do with his day. Now he had a purpose – to look after Norman. He had to walk him, feed him and play with him, but rather than feeling overwhelmed by the responsibility, Lorraine could see Oliver was enjoying caring for him.

Every morning, Oliver would take Norman on his walk. They had two or three different routes either along the promenade or round the local park.

He came in one morning with a proud look on his face.

'I said hello to all these dog owners and Norman and I stopped for a chat with them,' he said.

Lorraine was amazed. Because of Oliver's autism, he struggled with aimless chitchat and there had to be a specific purpose or topic to his conversation. He found it difficult to make friends and, before then, he never would have spoken to anyone that he didn't know.

Having Norman was helping him to socialize. Lorraine witnessed it for herself when they were out walking together along the seafront one day. They saw a woman with a West Highland terrier and Lorraine was surprised when Oliver went straight over to her.

'We've got a Westie too,' he told her, and they chatted about her dog for a while.

It was something Lorraine had never seen before. Norman

had given Oliver an inner confidence and also a common subject for him to talk to people about.

Some of their neighbour's relatives had just got a Westie puppy and Oliver came to Lorraine one afternoon when he knew they were visiting.

'I think we should introduce Norman to Boo,' he told her.

'That's a nice idea,' Lorraine smiled.

So Oliver took Norman outside and while he ran around with the new puppy, Oliver chatted to their neighbour's relatives. It was so nice for Lorraine to see. Even if all he talked to them about was Norman, she didn't care. It was good to see her son chatting to strangers off his own back – something he never would have done before. Norman had given him the confidence to want to go out and meet people and talk to them.

Both Lorraine and Oliver had been so worried about getting a dog that would react badly to Oliver's autism, but Norman took everything in his stride. If Oliver made a sudden movement or noise, Norman didn't even flinch and nothing seemed to faze him.

When Oliver got back from volunteering at the Amnesty store one lunchtime, Lorraine could sense that he was very upset.

'The till broke,' he told her.

He was very distressed and Lorraine could see that he was blaming himself.

'It's not your fault,' she told him. 'It broke because it's a very old till. No one is blaming you.'

But she could tell that Oliver was convinced it was because of something he'd done wrong. She could see that he'd held all of his upset in until he'd got home and now he was having an almighty anxiety attack.

She tried her best to reassure him but she knew that when Oliver was distressed and anxious, there was nothing she could do or say that would make any difference.

'It's my fault. It's my fault,' he repeated as he paced up and down the living room.

He started to cry and hit himself. Lorraine felt helpless. It was hard for her as a parent to witness it and not be able to do anything.

Norman had been curled up on the sofa, watching Oliver closely. Suddenly his ears pricked up and he could sense that something wasn't right. He got up, wandered over to Oliver and sat by his feet. He didn't do anything, he just sat there and stared up into Oliver's eyes as if he were telling him that he could feel his pain. Lorraine held her breath as Oliver immediately stopped ranting and looked down at Norman.

'Sorry Norman,' he said, bending down to give him a pat. 'I didn't mean to scare you. It's going to be OK.'

Within a few minutes, Oliver was much calmer. Lorraine watched in amazement as he lay down on the floor and Norman came and sat next to him and rolled onto his side so Oliver could rub his belly. Lorraine could practically see Oliver's anxiety levels drop as he stroked Norman's soft, fluffy white coat.

She couldn't reassure him, but Norman had an instant ability to comfort Oliver and bring him back into the moment. He had such a calming influence on him.

Norman provided that unconditional love Oliver had desperately wanted and needed. They spent the majority of the day together, hanging out. Oliver would walk and feed him and then they'd have a play. Norman loved running around the garden while Oliver threw the ball to him. When they were inside, his favourite game was tug of war. Oliver would hold one end of an industrial-strength length of rope and Norman would hold the other and they would see who was the strongest.

He provided Oliver with real companionship and he was such an easy dog to understand and be around. He was constantly ready for a play and a tummy rub. Oliver had always found it hard to relax but Norman was teaching him how.

A few months after they'd got him, *The Dog House* crew came to film them to see how they were getting on with Norman. They were sat on the sofa, talking to the camera, when Norman came into the room and ran straight up to Oliver. It was so natural and Lorraine could see their bond.

Since Covid, Oliver worried about Lorraine and where she was so she was reluctant to leave him. But now they've got

Norman, she knows Oliver will be OK. Norman gives Oliver the reassurance he needs to stop him from worrying.

Lorraine feels Norman helps keep her calm too. When he trots into the room with his floppy ear, that's enough to make her laugh. On an evening, Norman sits with her on the sofa. He's got arthritis in his legs, so now he has a special mini staircase that he climbs in order to sit next to Lorraine. He curls up next to her and she can feel herself instantly relax.

From being so worried about Oliver, Lorraine is now seeing little seeds of hope. He's back volunteering at Amnesty, he's enjoying going to the cinema and his running club has started up again. He's also having weekly counselling sessions which, along with Norman, are helping him manage his anxiety.

He's now doing all of this with his buddy Norman by his side.

Norman helped Oliver when he was at his lowest and most isolated, giving his life a purpose and also a sense of responsibility. He's his constant, most trusted companion – in fact Oliver describes him as his best friend in the whole world.

Lorraine can see the massive difference Norman has made to her son and the way that he calms him. She knows Oliver thinks Norman understands him and accepts him for who he is. They've got such a lovely relationship and bond. When she contacted Woodgreen, Lorraine never dreamed of finding such a perfect match. Oliver truly has found his best friend.

CHAPTER THREE

Obi

It was the high-pitched screeching that Mike couldn't forget. It was always there, continually going round and round in his head, ringing in his ears.

It was the noise that rockets made as they shot towards their target, right before they exploded on impact. And Mike couldn't stop thinking about the fact that sometimes that target could have been him.

'Are you OK?' his girlfriend Tracy asked, snapping him out of his thoughts.

Mike nodded.

They were having an ordinary evening sat on the sofa watching TV. Mike felt he couldn't tell her about the demons that he was continually fighting in his head. Or the vivid images that crept into his mind every night the minute he closed his eyes and tried to sleep.

He couldn't tell anyone because he knew no one would understand. It felt like everything that had happened to him in his past had well and truly come back to haunt him.

When Mike left school, he'd joined the Marines for seven years. After that, he'd ended up working all over the world as a contractor for security firms in Europe and the Middle East and had set up his own tourism business in Indonesia. He'd lived in some dangerous places including Afghanistan and Iraq.

Sadly in 2017 his marriage had broken down and he'd returned to live in the UK from Asia for the first time in eighteen years.

Mike had grown up in Belfast but he'd moved to South Yorkshire where his parents now lived. He had only been back in the UK for three months when he'd been offered another security job in Africa so he'd been backwards and forwards.

When that contract had ended in March 2019, Mike had decided to take a few months off to relax and work out what he wanted to do next with his life. But now, several months later, he knew that had been the worst decision that he'd ever made.

After living his life continually at 100 miles per hour, this was the first time Mike had had to properly think in years. It gave him time to reflect on all he'd gone through, all the dangerous situations that he'd been in and the close calls that he'd had. The stress of that, coupled with a flare-up of an old back injury he'd got during his stint in the Marines, was pushing him towards breaking point.

'What's wrong?' Tracy asked him. 'I know there's something, Mike.'

'I told you, I'm fine,' he snapped.

She knew something was up but Mike couldn't bring himself to tell her what he was really thinking about. He was actually going over and over the same day in his mind – the morning in Afghanistan when a rocket had almost killed him.

In 2014, Mike had been working as a contractor at a US military base that was constantly being hit. Every day he would hear the screech of rockets in the distance but he would crack on with work and try not to think about it. He knew the only time to worry was if the sirens went off. That signalled that a rocket was going to land in his part of the base and meant he had three seconds to hit the floor before impact. Thankfully it had never happened to him.

Every Saturday, Mike and one of colonels would go for an eight-mile run around the perimeter of the base, setting off at 5 a.m. before it got too hot. On this particular morning they'd only run a few hundred metres when they'd heard it.

It was a noise that everyone at the base knew, but Mike had never heard it this close before. It was so loud that it made his ears ring.

It was the high-pitched whistling that meant a rocket was about to come down on them. In a split second, Mike's life had flashed before him and he'd hit the ground, closed his eyes and prepared to die.

The screeching had got louder and louder.

Mike had heard and felt the almighty rumble as the rocket exploded on impact. He'd looked around in disbelief but both him and the colonel were still there, face down in the dirt without a scratch on them. Within seconds, people had swarmed around them checking they were OK.

'I'm absolutely fine,' Mike had told them, still in shock.

It was only when he stumbled to his feet that he'd realized what had happened. They had been running around the edge of the perimeter wall and, in a stroke of pure luck, the rocket had landed on the other side of it and they'd been protected from the blast.

Seconds later the sirens had gone off to signify that the danger had passed and they were all clear.

'Come on, let's carry on running,' Mike had said to the colonel, who was in his sixties and had had a long and distinguished military career.

He'd looked at Mike incredulously and said: 'That's the closest I've ever come to dying.'

A few weeks later, the colonel retired from service.

Like everything else that had happened in his life, Mike had just brushed it off. In the Marines, it had all been about goals, achievements and targets. He'd been trained, drilled and programmed. Mike didn't ever talk about his feelings, he pushed them to one side and got on with the job in hand. But now, years later, everything that he'd pushed away was swirling around in his mind and it was building up into the perfect storm.

'Talk to me,' begged Tracy. 'I know there's something wrong.'

But Mike couldn't. Suddenly everything he'd been through in the past came crashing down on top of him. It was like a train going at high speed before derailing and his whole life coming to a halt.

For the past few months, Mike hadn't been sleeping properly. Every night he closed his eyes, but his brain wouldn't allow him to rest. He would picture scenes from his life and replay them in his mind and have hot and cold sweats. Every morning he felt like a broken man.

Mike started drinking every day to try and numb the pain and knock himself out, but it didn't help. It worked for a brief moment and then it all came flooding back again. He started to push everyone away – his friends, his family and Tracy. She was a family friend and they had only been dating for a few months. Mike wouldn't have blamed her if she had ended the relationship and walked away but, much to his surprise, she had stuck by him.

One night Mike's dad invited them both along to a work reunion. Mike had always been the kind of man that would chat to everyone but now he stood in the corner with his head down, trying to avoid making eye contact with anyone.

Afterwards, his dad pulled him to one side.

'You were a bit cold and rude,' he told him. 'Whenever anybody talked to you, you gave them short, snappy answers.'

'I'm sorry Dad,' Mike replied. 'I'm not feeling myself.'

The truth was, he felt like a completely different person.

He was so caught up with fighting the demons inside his head that nothing else mattered. It was wrecking his and Tracy's relationship and they were arguing constantly. Mike was pushing the people closest to him away, but he couldn't help it. He was angry with everybody.

After months of insomnia, Mike reached his lowest point. He could see only one solution to make the pain stop and that was to end his life.

But every time that he hit the pits of despair, he forced himself to imagine his parents and Tracy crying over his coffin. He could see the heartache etched on their faces, the tears running down their cheeks. But Mike was in such a dark place, he worried that one day even that image wouldn't be enough to stop him.

Luckily Tracy could see how bad things had got and she phoned Mike's mum.

'Mike's in a really bad way and he needs help,' she told her.

They persuaded him to go to the doctor and tell him how he was feeling. With nothing else to lose, Mike opened up. It was the first time he'd talked about what he was going through to anyone and it was hard.

'It sounds like you've got complex PTSD,' the GP told him.

Complex post-traumatic stress disorder was triggered by a number of incidents rather than just one. Mike knew his marriage ending had caused a chain reaction of all the things that had been swirling around inside him for years that he'd buried until now. He was stuck, trapped in the past, and couldn't move forward.

Mike knew he needed professional help, so he started weekly counselling sessions.

At his first session, his counsellor pointed to the filing cabinet behind his desk.

'Imagine that cabinet is filled with what's in your head – all your life, all your memories, all your stresses, everything,' he told him. 'And somebody's come along and jumbled them all up – that's your head right now.'

He explained that what they were going to do during their sessions was slowly take the files out, analyze them, talk about the things inside them and then put everything back in the right order.

Mike thought it was a brilliant way to describe it and, over the next few months, that's exactly what he did.

Every week Mike turned up for his appointment, never missing a single one. For the first time in his life, he started to open up and he would cry in every session.

It was the hardest thing he'd ever done but thankfully it worked and after fourteen months of talking therapy and taking medication to help him sleep, Mike finally felt like he was on the road to recovery.

However, he still felt as if he needed something else to help him move on with his life. Something to give him a focus and a push in the right direction.

'I think I'm going to get a dog,' he told Tracy one day.

'That's a great idea,' she agreed.

They didn't live together and Tracy knew he sometimes struggled with the evenings when she wasn't there and he had too much time on his hands to think about the past.

A dog would keep him company and give him a focal point in his life. Every day she could see him getting stronger and happier but she thought a dog would really help him heal and bring him some much-needed joy and fun.

Mike was at his parents' house one day when his mum spotted an advert on social media.

'It's a TV show where they find people a rescue dog,' she told him. 'They make sure they match people with the right dog. They could help you.'

'I don't think so,' replied Mike, despondently.

But after much persuading from his parents, he finally gave in and emailed them.

Several weeks later, in August 2020, Mike and Tracy headed to Woodgreen. Mike explained about his PTSD diagnosis and everything that he'd been through.

'I've been having counselling for over a year now and it's teaching me so many things about how to deal with grief, fear and anger,' he said.

He told their dog-behaviour and training specialist Wendy about the kind of dog that he was looking for.

'I'd like something like a German shepherd or a Border collie,' he told her. 'I'd rather steer away from anything too boisterous.'

Mike had recently had an operation on his back and was struggling with an infection.

The staff racked their brains and eventually came up with an eleven-week-old red setter cross puppy called Obi.

Mike hadn't mentioned a puppy but they knew he had plenty of time on his hands and training him would give him a bit of a project.

Obi was a super-cute, fun dog who had come into Woodgreen after his owner's work patterns changed and they were going to be away from the house for long periods of time. They were hoping to find someone who was around a bit more and Mike seemed like the perfect match.

Wendy went to break the good news to Mike and Tracy.

'Obi is full of energy and loves to play,' she told them. 'He's affectionate too and is a real softie.'

When Mike asked what he was crossed with, he was surprised to hear it was a poodle.

'A poodle's not the kind of dog that I'd normally ever go for,' he said, but he was prepared to keep an open mind.

Neither of them was sure what Obi was going to look like but as soon as his handler carried him into the meeting pen, Tracy was sold.

'Oh he's beautiful,' she gasped as this little ball of chestnut-coloured fluff scampered towards them. 'I love him.'

Mike couldn't stop smiling. He could tell Obi was a bit of a handful as he started eating soil out of a plant pot and he had to fish a stone out of his mouth.

'I think he's a mischievous little fella,' he grinned.

He wanted an active dog but he also wanted an affectionate one and Mike wasn't sure whether Obi would fit the bill.

He got down on his knees and called Obi over to him. He bolted straight to Mike and jumped up at him, covering his face with licks and kisses. Then he rolled onto his back and let Mike stroke his belly.

Tracy could instantly see the look of joy on Mike's face.

'You're smitten, aren't you?' she said.

He nodded.

'Yep,' he said. 'He's lovely.'

Obi had stolen both their hearts and Mike felt an instant connection to him.

He knew he couldn't say no to this gorgeous pup. 'You've found your daddy,' Mike told him.

Three weeks later, Mike brought Obi home. He lived in a town house and as soon as Obi ran through the front door, he bolted around all three floors like a hurricane.

As he was only a puppy, he wasn't fully house-trained. Mike had thought he was prepared. He'd covered all of the floors with countless puppy pads but Obi managed to find the tiniest patch that wasn't covered to wee on.

He was much more hyper than Mike had expected and he ran excitedly from room to room. Mike spent the first day chasing him around and cleaning wee off the carpets. His back was still sore from surgery and the subsequent infection so physically it was hard.

'It's a battle of wills,' he told Tracy. 'He's trying to break me and I'm trying to break him.'

By the evening, Mike was exhausted and he prayed Obi would settle OK. He wanted him to have the run of the house and go wherever he liked so he put a crate downstairs with a bed inside it with the door open, a bed on the middle floor and one on the top floor. That way, Obi could choose to sleep where he was most comfortable.

However, as he lay in bed that night, Mike could hear bangs and crashes and he could tell Obi was still running about.

He heaved himself out of bed, his back aching, to go and check on him.

Obi didn't seem to realize it was after midnight and he was still full of beans, tearing around the house, jumping on the beds and doing 360-degree donuts. Much to his dismay, Mike saw that he'd weed everywhere again too and he'd already run out of carpet shampoo.

His heart sank. Could he really cope with this or had he bitten off more than he could chew? Mike had always said he didn't want a dog that was too boisterous but Obi was hyperactive and he was struggling to keep up with him.

He loved Obi but was it case of the right dog but the wrong time?

Finally by 2.30 a.m. he had settled down to sleep.

The next day he told Tracy his fears.

'I'm worried he's too much for me,' he told her.

'He's just being a normal puppy,' she reassured him. 'You don't have kids and give them back do you? You have to persevere.'

Mike knew she was right and it would be worth it in the end. Obi was in a new place and he was probably feeling stressed and unsure.

The next few weeks were a battle. Every waking hour was spent feeding Obi, walking him and taking him to puppy-training classes.

Mike discovered the best way to deal with his incessant energy was to try and tire him out. As the days passed, they slowly started to slip into a routine. In the morning, Mike would get up at 5.30 a.m. and give Obi his breakfast, then they'd go out for a long walk for up to an hour. Every two hours throughout the day, he would take him out and do the same thing. They went to the cricket field near Mike's house up to five times a day.

It was exhausting, but Mike liked the fact that his days had some structure to them; he was used to it from being in the military. He enjoyed the familiarity and the routine and he could tell that Obi did too.

His whole life had been turned upside down by this puppy, who seemed more like a toddler, but he was enjoying the responsibility.

At the end of one day, Mike flopped down on the sofa, absolutely exhausted. He realized that Obi had consumed his entire day from morning through to night. But because everything was about Obi, he hadn't had a chance to think about anything else. The negative thoughts that had crept into his mind and affected him in the past were still there but with Obi around he didn't have time to dwell on them.

'Are you OK?' Tracy asked him when she called him. 'You sound shattered.'

'I've got Obi to thank for that,' laughed Mike. 'He's run me ragged.'

He was so tired by the end of each day, he was sleeping better too.

Mike really enjoyed taking Obi to puppy-training classes. He started to see Obi's personality shine through and he could tell that he was smart. When he led him onto the field, Obi sat there, very straight and regal, watching the other dogs.

'We're going to try and teach recall today,' the instructor told them.

While the other dogs struggled to follow instructions, Obi got it straight away and Mike was so proud of him.

The training gave him a laugh too. It was always so funny when the dogs were trying to grasp a new concept and everything went wrong and descended into chaos.

It gave Mike something to focus on and occupy his mind and he loved seeing how Obi was progressing.

It definitely started to work. As the months passed, Obi became much more settled and calm. Within a few weeks he'd cracked toilet-training and at night, he'd curl up in a ball on Mike's bed. If Mike woke up in the early hours or he couldn't sleep, he loved looking down and seeing Obi in his favourite sleeping position – lying on his back with his legs in the air. It never failed to make him smile and it was a constant comfort having Obi there.

As time passed, Mike bumped into more and more people on his daily dog walks with Obi. He was out so many times each day, there was always somebody around.

Every morning at 6 a.m. he and Obi were out on the cricket field with a training lead.

It was the prime time for other dog walkers. One day a woman came over to them with her dog.

'What a beautiful puppy,' she said. 'What breed is he?'

Mike chatted to her for a while, then he'd only walked for another few minutes when someone else stopped him.

'I see you out here every day,' the man told him. 'Your dog always looks so happy.'

Mike explained how he was trying to train him.

'Where's your accent from?' the man asked. 'I can tell you're not from round here.'

Before he knew it, Mike was telling him his life story.

Obi loved his walks too and he enjoyed meeting other dogs. He was so soft and gentle. If a small dog barked, he jumped a mile, and he'd lie on his back on the grass and let two or three other dogs jump over him. While Obi tore around with his canine friends, Mike chatted to their owners.

'I think I've spoken to everyone in the village this morning,' he told Tracy when she came round later. 'I know all the dogs' names but I don't think I'll remember all the people's.'

She was so pleased. When Mike had been in the worst grip of his PTSD he hadn't wanted to speak to anyone and she was amazed to hear that he was opening up and talking to complete strangers. Even a few months ago that would have been unthinkable and it showed her how far Mike had come. He recognized it too and rather than feeling forced, it felt really natural.

'I know I was a closed book,' he told Tracy. 'I was so trapped inside my own head, I couldn't communicate with anyone else.'

For months, Mike hadn't wanted to go out and if he did, he'd walked along with his head down. Since he'd moved back to the UK he didn't know anyone in his local area but now, because of Obi, he started to feel part of a community.

Each walk they went on, someone stopped him to ask what breed Obi was or how old he was. Obi forced him to get out of the house and be sociable and Mike found he was really enjoying it. It felt good to be able to chat and laugh with people again and he felt more like his old self.

'I think Obi's helping to bring you out of your shell,' Tracy told him.

PTSD had changed Mike's whole personality to the extent that he'd been emotionless and reserved for so long. Now being able to talk to people again, to want to go out and to walk with his head held high felt like such a gift.

When their episode of *The Dog House* aired, he and Obi became local celebrities – although people tended to recognize Obi more than Mike. Strangers came up to talk to him in the street and to fuss over Obi who loved the attention.

Mike was out for a walk one day when an elderly lady walked up to him.

'Is this Obi?' she asked.

'It sure is,' smiled Mike.

'I thought I recognized you both from the TV,' she said.
She paused.

'Your story really moved me,' she continued. 'You see, my son had PTSD but unfortunately he didn't make it.'

Mike was gobsmacked and he struggled to hold back the tears as she told him how her son had taken his own life.

'Thank you for raising awareness of PTSD,' she told him.

'So many people still don't really understand how badly it affects people.'

Mike told her how well he was doing now and how much Obi had helped him.

'That's good to hear,' she said. 'You take care of yourself.'

Their encounter was so unexpected and Mike was incredibly moved that this woman had stopped to talk to him. He knew that he was one of the lucky ones. He was still here, moving forwards and enjoying life after things had felt so bleak for so long.

After a few months of having Obi, Mike couldn't imagine life without him. He was so loveable, and he wanted to be everyone's friend. They were like two peas in a pod and Obi was constantly glued to his side.

Mike was sat on the sofa one evening looking at his phone when Obi jumped up and lay down beside him. Mike felt a paw on his arm as Obi clawed away at his wrist.

'Obi no,' scolded Mike, getting back to his phone.

When Obi did the same thing again a few minutes later, Mike realized that he just wanted his attention. The minute he put his phone down, Obi rested his head on his leg.

He had a strong personality and he loved a joke. At home, Mike always lay on the four-seater sofa and Tracy sat on the smaller two-seater. One evening, she got up to go and get a glass of water from the kitchen. As soon as she left the room, Obi jumped up off the floor, ran over to the two-seater and lay down on it. When Tracy came back in, he wouldn't let her sit down so she went over to the bigger sofa where Mike was.

'Move over and I'll sit down here with you,' she told him.

Mike did as she'd asked but before she could sit down, Obi quickly leapt into her spot.

'He knows exactly what he's doing,' laughed Mike.

Obi was always great fun and he constantly made them both smile. He was their shadow and he wanted to do everything that they did. Whenever Mike brushed his teeth, he had to brush Obi's at the same time. If Tracy was putting mascara on, she had to pretend to put some on Obi too.

Mike hardly ever left Obi but if he did and came back into the house, Obi would always greet him in the same way. Mike would drop to his knees and Obi put his paws on his shoulders and Mike had to give him a back massage.

He made every day fun and Mike loved being around him.

At the height of his PTSD, evenings were always the hardest time of the day for Mike. When he was desperate to relax and switch off, his mind would start to wander and he would think about the past and all of the things that had gone wrong in his life. He had felt like there was a permanent grey cloud hanging over his head.

Evenings were a lot busier now he had Obi. If Mike was lying on the sofa, Obi would bring his ball to him and he'd spend an hour playing catch.

The negative thoughts occasionally still crept up on Mike.

One night he sat there and thought about his marriage ending and all the things he could have done differently.

It still felt very raw and he found his eyes filling with tears. Obi was lying next to him and, as if he sensed something was wrong, he placed his paw gently on Mike's leg. Mike smiled and looked into his big brown puppy eyes. He wrapped his arms round him and gave him a hug and Obi nuzzled into him.

'I love you Obi,' he told him. 'Thank you for being there.'

For Tracy, it was also a relief. She would always worry when she left Mike at home alone in the evenings. Now Obi was around, she could relax and know that he would be OK. She could tell the bad days were over and Mike didn't get stressed any more. He would spend his evenings hanging out with Obi then he would go to bed, shattered but happy, and drift off to sleep.

Mike still can't believe how far he's come in the past couple of years and he knows so much of that is down to Obi. Getting a dog has done more for him than he could ever have imagined and his attitude and outlook on life has completely changed. Every day he wakes up with Obi by his side and feels lucky for everything that he has.

Obi has helped to heal him and allowed him to move forwards. Without him, Mike believes it would have been a much longer and harder journey. PTSD is the toughest battle that he's ever had to deal with in his life, but Obi keeps him focused and busy. Thanks to Obi, Mike is a more compassionate person, and Obi has broken down Mike's barriers so he's more open and can talk to people. He's the best friend Mike could ever have asked for.

Sue Ketland, Woodgreen Canine Behaviour and Training Specialist

Sue Ketland glanced around her house. Wherever she looked, there was a dog. One was asleep on the kitchen floor, a couple were curled on the sofa, one was upstairs and another one was outside running around in the garden.

For Sue and her husband, Ritt, dogs were their family. They'd never wanted children and whenever Sue had felt broody, she'd taken in another rescue dog. Now they had five – a German shepherd called Lara who was the matriarch of their pack, Squidgy, a Border collie, Mush the Jack Russell and Nanuq and Reef who were both Australian shepherds.

Life with five dogs was an endless round of feeding, walking and training. It was chaos but Sue loved it. There was always a dog somewhere in the house and they even had a dog flap so they could let themselves out into the garden whenever they wanted.

Sue had always loved animals and she'd grown up with a spaniel called Cindy. When she had left school at sixteen, she didn't know what she wanted to do so she'd ended up getting a job in an accounts office.

Every morning, Sue would wake up and cry at the thought of going to work.

'I hate it,' she'd told her mum Nita.

'You need to get yourself a job working with animals,' her mum had said.

She knew how much Sue loved all animals because she'd save up her pocket money before spending it on feeding a colony of feral cats on their estate, or some wild birds and hedgehogs. Sue knew she didn't want to be a vet or a veterinary nurse as she was too squeamish to work in the medical side of things, but eventually her mum had found her a place on a Youth Training Scheme (YTS) in Animal Care.

As part of that, she had a work placement at Woodgreen which wasn't far from her home in Peterborough.

Sue had loved being with the dogs and learning about different breeds and their behaviour, how to read their body language and how to communicate with them. When the course had ended, she'd been delighted when Woodgreen had offered her a job and she's still there thirty-two years later.

Sue had been deputy head of the dog section for a few years and now she was working in dog behaviour and training. When she'd first started, she'd worked in the kennels – feeding, cleaning, walking and playing with the dogs. She'd then moved over to rehoming and had loved matching the dogs with new owners.

Working with dogs every day, there was no way Sue wasn't going to get one of her own. When she was still living at home, she'd nagged and nagged her mum until a few months later when her mum had finally relented and Sue had adopted her first rescue dog – a Border collie puppy called Sophie.

She was only twelve weeks old and very lively. Sue didn't have a clue at that stage about the differences in behaviour between breeds and that collies needed lots of exercise and mental stimulation. Sophie was a real handful and, much to her mum's annoyance, had even chewed a hole in the plaster-board walls at home.

'That's it,' she had sighed. 'You either get this dog properly trained or she'll have to go back to Woodgreen.'

There was no way Sue was going to let that happen so she'd thrown herself into training Sophie and had absolutely loved it. She'd enjoyed it so much, Sophie had ended up going to obedience shows and she was even a member of the Woodgreen agility team. For Sue, it had created a life-long interest in training dogs.

Sue was thirty and still working at Woodgreen when she'd met Ritt through a friend. He was a massive animal lover too but he'd lived in a flat at the time so he'd only had room for pet rats. But as soon as they'd moved in together six months later, their canine family had quickly grown. Sue's mum had fallen in love with Sophie by then and when Sue had left home, she wasn't allowed to take her.

Ritt's dream dog was a white long-haired German shepherd. Sue was working at Woodgreen one day when a five-month-old white German shepherd puppy had come into the rescue. She looked like a little polar bear and Sue had called Ritt straight away.

'Hello babe you'll never guess what's just come in,' she'd told him.

Within half an hour, he'd gone to Woodgreen to meet her and he had taken her straight away. Even though Lara had been parented by both Sue and Ritt she was definitely Ritt's dog and the pair of them had an amazingly close relationship.

Over the years, they'd rehomed another three dogs together but Ritt was still keen to rehome another one.

'Lara's getting old and I want a dog that she will have some influence over,' he told Sue. Lara mothered all the other dogs and disciplined them when it was needed.

They had got Nanuq from a breeder who had identified

when he was a few weeks old that he was going to grow into a challenging dog. The breeder had known he needed a highly experienced owner so she'd contacted Sue to see if she would consider taking him on. Then the same breeder had offered them another Australian shepherd called Reef who needed specialist care.

'She's got two mangled back feet and may have mobility problems in the future,' she'd told them.

Reef's mum had been over-zealous in her cleaning and had chewed half her back feet off.

'Please can we take her?' Ritt had begged, and even though it would take them to five dogs, Sue didn't need much persuading.

Australian shepherds were one of her favourite breeds and she loved their piercing blue eyes and unusual colouring. Nanuq was a blue merle, a mixture of grey, black and white that almost looked like marble, with a white and copper trim. Reef was a gorgeous red colour with a cream and white trim.

Reef had joined them and their family had grown to seven. At six months, she'd had reconstructive surgery on her back feet and thankfully from then on, they didn't cause her any more problems.

All their love went on their dogs, who were a big part of their lives. Sue and Ritt liked nothing more than walking in the countryside, chucking balls to the dogs while they ran freely.

At weekends, Ritt would stay at home gaming while Sue took the dogs to competitions. She loved the partnership that training them brought and that trust and bond you created with them. It was a deeper bond than just the companionship between owner and dog. When Sue trained a dog, they knew each other inside out and it really deepened her relationship with that animal.

Sue's first dog Sophie had been in an agility display team, Mush her Jack Russell was a comedy trick dog and now Squidgy, Reef and Nanuq were all competition obedience dogs.

By December 2013, sadly they only had two out of their five dogs. Lara had passed away first from old age. Sue and Ritt had her put down at home and after the vet had gone, they let the other dogs into the room, one at a time, to pay their respects. Mush came in first and gave her a little kiss goodbye and then jumped up onto the armchair. Squidgy followed and gave her a sad low tail wag and jumped up onto the sofa. Nanuq and Reef came in and gave her a goodbye sniff. There was a real sadness from all the dogs but also a slight element of relief because Lara had been the bossy one who had kept them all in line.

Squidgy had sadly died after getting to the ripe old age of fourteen and a half, and then Mush had wanted a quiet life in her retirement so she'd gone to live with Ritt's parents at their cottage by the sea.

There was also a lingering sadness for Sue and Ritt. They'd had five dogs for four years, and it had been chaos. There had never been a moment's peace and the house felt eerily quiet without their full pack. But they'd tried to focus on the positives and it meant they could give more time and attention to their two remaining dogs – Australian shepherds Reef and Nanuq. At about the same time, Sue could see Ritt wasn't well. He was bloated and had pain in his stomach. He'd feel really hungry but then he'd have only a few mouthfuls of food and feel full. He was also losing weight. Just before Christmas, the pain got worse and he was rushed to hospital with suspected appendicitis. Scans showed there was nothing wrong with his appendix so he had more tests.

In the New Year, Sue went with him to get the results.

'Unfortunately it's pancreatic cancer,' the consultant told them. 'I'm very sorry but it's already spread and I'm afraid it's terminal.'

Sue was hit by total shock and devastation. He was only thirty-eight. They'd planned to grow old together and travel the world but, in a matter of seconds, their future had been cruelly snatched away from them.

She looked over at Ritt. She could see a glimmer of fear in his eyes but even though it must have been the hardest thing in the world to hear, he remained stoic.

Sue in comparison went to pieces. By the time they got home, she was hysterical.

As Sue turned the key in the lock and pushed open the front door, Nanuq and Reef came running. Their world had been shattered but their dogs didn't know that and they danced around them like they always did, happy that they were back. It made Sue realize that life carried on and whatever the future held, they had to as well.

They stood in the kitchen, both shell-shocked.

'There's something I need to ask you,' Ritt said, putting his hands on her shoulders.

She looked into his eyes.

'Please don't cry,' he told her. 'I hate to see you cry because it makes me feel like I'm hurting you and I can't stand that.'

Sue nodded. From then on, there were lots of tears but she never ever cried in front of Ritt again.

Over the next few months, Sue watched, helpless, as Ritt went through chemotherapy and radiotherapy. It was hard to see how the treatment ravaged his body and made him so sick.

Even though he was in constant pain, he was always so brave and Sue never once saw him shed a tear. She could tell he was wrestling with the knowledge that he was going to die but she never heard him say 'why me?'

Sue knew she had to stay strong for him but she was struggling to cope and wasn't sleeping. She carried on working at Woodgreen but every morning she headed off to work feeling guilty that she wasn't spending time with Ritt. She didn't know how much time she had left with him and every moment was precious. She broke down several times at work and her concerned colleagues persuaded her to see the GP.

Seven months after his diagnosis, she was signed off with stress. It was the toughest time of Sue's life but Nanuq and Reef kept her going. Whatever else was going on, they still needed feeding, walking and love.

One day Ritt was curled up on the sofa, sleeping, after the chemotherapy had made him sick. The dogs needed a walk so she left him to rest. They were lucky enough to live in a village so within a few minutes, she was surrounded by open countryside. It was the first time that Sue had been out of the house all day and as she threw a ball for the dogs, she felt her shoulders sag.

She knew Ritt was going through so much and was being unbelievably courageous. But it was hard for her too seeing the person she loved go through so much pain and suffering.

It was a relief to be out of the house with the dogs and clear her head before she had to go back home and face reality again.

Sue stood in the middle of the field and burst into tears. Reef, who always seemed to know how Sue was feeling, ran over to her and nudged her hand with her nose.

'It's OK girl,' she sobbed. 'Mummy's just having a sad moment.'

This escape from the house was also her time to cry.

She'd kept her promise to Ritt and he'd never seen her upset. Walking the dogs was her way of recharging so she could go home and face whatever came next.

When they got back, Ritt was still asleep. Reef, his most loyal girl, curled up next to him on the sofa with her head gently resting on his knee. She was always so sensitive and intuitive and she knew instinctively when he needed comfort and extra cuddles.

Nanuq had always been a bit of a handful but after Ritt's diagnosis, Sue noticed even he seemed to realize something had changed and he toned down his behaviour.

Eighteen months after his diagnosis, Sue could see Ritt was getting weaker. He wanted to die at home and Sue had promised him that that would happen. He was permanently upstairs in bed now with two morphine drivers in his arm.

During the day, both dogs would curl up on the bed with him and Reef wouldn't leave his side. In between hours of sleep, he would get so much comfort waking up and seeing them there.

It was such an unreal, intense time for Sue. During the day, Ritt's family would come and spend time with him and district nurses would call and check his medication. At night, the local hospice arranged for night nurses to come and sit with him while Sue tried to get some sleep.

She was so scared of losing Ritt but the dogs brought her constant comfort.

Nanuq had a thick fluffy coat so he preferred to sleep on the cool Lino in the kitchen but every night Reef would curl up in bed with her.

'You know something's wrong don't you girl,' Sue told her and with Reef by her side, somehow she felt less alone.

In September 2015, twenty months after he was diagnosed, Ritt died at home with Sue by his side. She felt numb with shock and grief.

The idea of the dogs thinking Ritt had just disappeared and left them broke her heart. So after the undertakers had been to take his body away, she let Reef and Nanuq into their bedroom to sniff the bed in the hope that they would somehow understand what had happened.

Whether they did or not, over the next few weeks they were very clingy, always there with cuddles and kisses. After Ritt's funeral and the constant stream of visitors, Sue could sense that both dogs were relieved that the house was quiet again and they could get back to their normal routine. But Sue knew life for her was never going to be the same again.

Ritt was gone and, as far as she was concerned, her future had died with him too. What was the point in her being here if he wasn't?

Sue was curled up in bed one morning when the alarm went off. She pulled the duvet around her as a wave of grief hit her all over again like it did every morning when she remembered.

Ritt was dead.

The tears started to flow. Then suddenly Sue heard a rustling. A furry head appeared at one side of the bed.

Nanuq.

Then one at the other side.

'Hello Reef,' she mumbled.

They both jumped up on the bed and before she knew it, they'd lain down beside her and started licking her tears away. Despite her upset, Sue couldn't help but smile.

'Thank you,' she told them. 'What would I do without you two?'

Every morning, Reef jumped up on the bed with Sue's slipper in her mouth, willing her to get up. She made the noise that Sue called the 'woo woos' – a cross between a bark and a yodel that was her way of saying good morning and showing Sue that she was happy.

Without Ritt, Sue wanted to give up and stay in bed all day but the dogs wouldn't let her. They gave her a purpose. Even though her husband had gone, she still had her doggy children who needed her to care for them. As far as they were concerned, life went on and they still needed feeding and walking. They needed someone to stroke them and throw them a ball and they forced Sue to keep going.

The dogs gave her day structure too. So many times in those dark early days she had the urge to just get in her car and drive until she ran out of petrol, to escape. But she had two little faces staring at her saying, 'Hey Mummy throw us a tennis ball.' Or 'Let's have a cuddle or go for walk.'

Despite Sue's overwhelming sadness and grief, they still manage to make her laugh, especially Nanuq who had a sweet, funny side to him.

Sue was sat on the sofa one night with a glass of cola next to her. Nanuq wanted her to play ball with him but she was engrossed in a TV programme. The next thing she knew, Nanuq came trotting over to her and carefully dropped his tennis ball into her glass of cola.

Sue couldn't help but laugh.

'Did Daddy tell you to do that?' she smiled.

She could just imagine how Ritt would have laughed if he'd been there to see that.

As the months passed, Sue could see that her friends and family were desperate for her to be OK and to start moving on.

'How are you doing?' a friend asked her one day when she rang.

'Oh I'm OK,' Sue told her because she knew that was what her friend wanted to hear.

But when she put the phone down she burst into tears. She wasn't OK.

'I miss him,' she told the dogs.

They were the only people in the world she could talk

honestly to about how she truly felt. They didn't judge her and loved her unconditionally. She sat on the sofa with them and had a cry.

Sometimes Sue would watch those videos on social media of military personnel returning from deployment. There was a compilation of different front doors opening and their dogs greeting them after they'd been away for months. Sue always shed a tear when she watched them and she couldn't help but think how Nanuq and Reef would react if Ritt suddenly walked through their front door.

What she wouldn't give to see him or hear his voice one more time.

It was two long years before Sue felt as if she could start to live her life again without Ritt. She could never truly move on but with Reef and Nanuq by her side, she could try to move forwards.

One of the ways that Sue coped was by throwing herself into her work. For many years, she'd helped to train the staff at Woodgreen in animal behaviour but recently they had started giving members of the public who were struggling with their dogs advice too.

Sue knew many of the issues people had with their animals were down to a lack of education and she loved saving relationships.

A man called her one day, nearly in tears about the problems he was having with his rescue Border collie.

'I think I've made a terrible mistake taking her on,' he told Sue. 'I'm thinking about giving her up.'

He explained that he'd had collies before and he knew they needed lots of exercise and mental stimulation, but this dog was becoming more and more withdrawn and was terrified of him.

'You need to take the pressure off, back off and let this dog relax,' Sue told him. 'He needs to get used to you and the house in his own time.'

She encouraged him to take it really slowly and steadily. Sue spoke to him every week for nearly two months and over that time, he was amazed at the dog's transformation. As soon as he took the pressure off and left the dog to his own devices, their relationship grew and grew.

'He's just awesome and I love him,' he told Sue.

She got such a sense of satisfaction when it worked. She'd helped restore a relationship between an owner and their dog and prevent the dog from going into a rescue.

She loved talking to dog owners who were having all sorts of problems. She wasn't there to judge. She was there to talk to them and advise them and explain.

By the time *The Dog House* started filming, Sue had been working at Woodgreen for thirty years and was one of the longest serving members of staff.

In the first series, one of the people that Sue had to find a dog for was a pensioner called Alan whose wife Brenda had recently died of cancer. He was lonely and hoped getting a dog would help bring him some comfort.

It struck a nerve with Sue as her experience of losing Ritt was still quite raw. He was such a kind, gentle man and Sue was determined to do her best for him as she knew first-hand how much dogs could help someone after a loss.

She matched him with a nine-year-old Lhasa cross called Ruby, who had come into Woodgreen after her owner had died.

As Sue watched them meet for the first time in the pen, she held her breath.

Please let it work, she willed.

Ruby wouldn't go to Alan at first but then she did. Much to Sue's delight, this man remembered everything that she'd told him about the dog – how she liked her ears to be stroked and not to overwhelm her.

Sue had tears in her eyes as she watched them together.

'Oh it's wonderful,' she smiled. 'They're made for each other.'

It was a really touching story and she loved helping this grieving man to find the perfect dog.

In December 2019, Sue became worried about Nanuq. He was losing weight rapidly despite having a good appetite and he'd started stumbling a little bit. He was almost thirteen and Sue could see that his body was failing him.

'I'm afraid it looks like he has cancer,' the vet said after examining him.

Sue didn't want to put him through a barrage of tests at his age. She had a couple of lovely days with him at home and then she held him in her arms as the vet put him to sleep. As she'd done before, afterwards she let Reef into the room to say her goodbye. She gave his body a goodbye sniff then she cuddled into Sue. She and Nanuq had been inseparable and Sue could see she was devastated.

Over the next few days, Reef was very quiet and lost. She and Sue comforted each other in their grief. She was such a sensitive dog and so in tune with what Sue was feeling. As she'd done after Ritt had died, she'd snuggle into Sue and lick her tears away.

It felt so strange to Sue only having one dog but she and Reef were best buddies. They were so close and supported each other through lockdown. Eighteen months later, in August 2021, Reef was diagnosed with a tumour. It was already too big to treat and Sue had to make the devastating decision to have her put to sleep. She'd got so ill so quickly that Sue had to make a decision there and then, and she didn't want to prolong her pain.

She was able to spend some time with her at the vet beforehand.

'You go and see Daddy and your brothers and sisters, and I'll see you all again one day,' Sue told her as she hugged and kissed her goodbye.

For the first time ever, Sue didn't have a dog in her life.

Reef had felt like her last connection to Ritt and now she had gone too.

Even after Ritt's death, the house had never felt truly empty because she still had Reef and Nanuq, but now she was truly alone.

Everything reminded her of Reef. Sue was making dinner one night when, out of habit, she dropped a handful of frozen peas. It was only as they hit the floor that she realized Reef wasn't there any more to hoover them up. Reef used to love frozen peas and Sue always used to, accidentally on purpose, spill some on the floor for her to gobble up.

As Sue got out the dustpan and brush to clear them up, tears rolled down her face. Everywhere she looked in the house, there were the empty places where Reef should have been and she couldn't bear to clear her water bowl away. It was strange getting out the shower and not having her there waiting for her outside the bathroom door or in the empty armchair on the landing where she used to curl up. It was even strange when the postman knocked at the door and there was no barking.

Sue doesn't know if she will ever get another dog but she's keeping an open mind. It was something she used to do with Ritt and it feels like a big step to do it on her own. For now, she's enjoying spending her days at work surrounded by dogs and she's trying to embrace her new-found freedom and travel.

Dogs have always been there for her and without them, she knew she wouldn't have even got out of bed for weeks after Ritt died. They really have saved her life.

CHAPTER FOUR

Rocky

Coronavirus might have put an end to their May half-term holiday plans but Tula Coxon was determined that if they couldn't make it to Mallorca, then Mallorca would come to them. So, in a bid to cheer up her sons, thirteen-year-old Alfie and eleven-year-old Dan, Tula and her husband Russell had created what they called 'fake Mallorca' in their back garden in South Wales.

Now the sun was shining, the padding pool was full and if they closed their eyes, they could just about convince themselves that they were on a Spanish island.

But as she looked over at Dan, splashing around in the pool in his swimming shorts, she was horrified by what she saw. His ribs were sticking out, his stomach was hollow and he looked like a skeleton.

Six months ago, life had changed when Tula's eldest son Jay had moved over 200 miles away to start a carpentry apprenticeship in Cheshire. Living with three boys, things were always boisterous and chaotic and they'd got used to the constant noise and mess. Then Jay had left and suddenly the house felt empty and eerily quiet.

The person who'd taken Jay's departure the hardest had been Dan. He'd always been a little bit different to other children and Tula constantly worried about him. He reached every developmental milestone much later than his older brothers and rather than playing with other children, he preferred to stay by her side. His speech was delayed and as he got older, it was tricky for people to understand what he was saying. Jay had been Dan's protector and he'd spoken for him when Dan didn't have a voice. Before she'd met Russell, Tula had been a single parent for many years and while she went off to work each morning, teenager Jay got Dan up and ready for school, gave him his breakfast and helped him into his school uniform. They were very close and when Jay had left home, Dan missed his eldest brother terribly.

Dan had always been a fussy eater but after Jay left, there were only one or two things that he would eat. He'd never had a big appetite but his portions had gradually got even smaller. One evening Tula sat with him at the dinner table after everyone else had finished. He ate painfully slowly, chewing every mouthful over and over again. It took him two long, frustrating hours to eat two chicken dippers.

'What is it Dan?' she'd begged him. 'Please tell me what's wrong.'

That's when he'd admitted that he was frightened to eat because he was anxious that it was going to make him ill. He was worried that he was going to be sick or choke. Sometimes he would chew his food for ages and then spit it out into a tissue because he was too scared to swallow it.

Tula was shocked. She was desperate to help her son but the hard thing was, she couldn't force him to eat. She'd done everything that she could to encourage him – given him the same types of food that she knew he liked day after day, even if it meant he existed on a diet of pepperoni pizza, chicken dippers and digestive biscuits and praised him when he'd managed a few mouthfuls.

A few months later, in March 2020, coronavirus had spread throughout the world and the entire country had been forced to go into lockdown. His added fears about the global pandemic meant that Dan was even more anxious and his eating had got progressively worse. Tula began to dread mealtimes and they had become a battle of wills. As soon as she put the food on the table, she could see the telltale signs of Dan's anxiety kicking in. His breathing would get shallow and he started making little clicking noises. In his head, he'd convinced himself that if he ate, he was going to get ill. Every mouthful was torture and it would end with everyone feeling sad, frustrated and stressed.

Tula knew Dan had lost some weight but she hadn't realized just how much until now. Seeing him stood there in the paddling pool in his swimming shorts, his skin hanging off his bones, she was both horrified and scared. Her son was wasting away in front of her.

She rang the GP and they advised her to take Dan straight to hospital. The doctors were as shocked by how he looked as much as she was, and they were worried that something was seriously wrong. At one point, they suggested a brain problem and they even suspected it could be leukemia. Over the next few months, Dan had endless tests, scans and X-rays but thankfully they couldn't find anything physical that was preventing him from eating. The cause was purely psychological.

He was severely underweight for his age and the doctors warned her that if he lost any more then he'd have to be fed through a tube. Tula was devastated. She knew that if Dan had a feeding tube fitted, he would quickly become reliant on it and the risk was he would never eat normally again. The thought of him being dependent on being tube-fed for the rest of his life was unbearable. He had to put some weight on and quickly.

The hospital put him on meal replacement milkshakes and gradually they started to work. Dan gained over a stone and Tula was relieved that he was back on track.

But after a few weeks he said the milkshakes were making him feel sick and he refused to have them any more. Much to Tula's despair, he started to lose the weight that he'd put back on.

One night, Alfie came to her.

'I've just seen Dan on his iPad looking up different breeds of dog,' he told her. 'Please can we get a dog Mum? I really think it would help him.'

The boys had been begging her to get a dog for years although Russell wasn't keen. But maybe a dog could be the answer to Dan's problems? If he had to look after and feed a dog then maybe he would start to realize that he had to feed himself too. Tula knew that Dan's issues around eating were triggered by anxiety and dogs were good at relieving stress and helping people relax. Dan obviously thought it was a good idea and Alfie did too and Tula could work on Russell. A dog would also bring some much-needed fun to their house and give them that lift they all needed since Jay had left and they were plunged into lockdown.

Trapped in the depths of despair and worry about her youngest son, Tula was willing to try anything right now. However, she soon learnt that finding a dog when you didn't have any prior knowledge is a minefield. She was also terrified about getting it wrong. If she didn't choose a suitable breed then there was a risk it would make Dan even more stressed and worried.

One day she came across a video clip on Facebook. It was from an episode in the first series of the *The Dog House* where an elderly widower whose wife had died had adopted a dog to keep him company. It led her to the Woodgreen page where she saw they were looking for participants for the new series. Could they help her find the perfect dog for Dan?

After several emails and video chats, she was shocked but ecstatic to be told they were going to take part in the show.

With Russell still in denial, in August 2020 they drove the 250 miles from their home in Porthcawl to Woodgreen. The night before their visit, they checked into a hotel and ordered takeaway pizzas. As they all tucked in, the boys chatted away excitedly about the dog they were hopefully going to be matched with the following day.

It was only when Tula was clearing away the boxes that she realized Dan had eaten three slices of pizza – the most he'd ever eaten. Just the thought of getting a dog had been enough to encourage her son to eat and she was filled with hope.

On a swelteringly hot day, the family headed to Woodgreen filled with excitement and nerves and, for Tula, an underlying sense of fear. Could the Dog House team rise to the challenge and help find them the perfect dog or was Dan going to be left bitterly disappointed?

As they chatted to pet advisor Helen, they explained they were very open about breeds.

'Personality is more important for us,' Tula told her. 'We'd like a dog who is calm and chilled.'

Their only physical criteria came from Alfie.

'I want a big dog that can swim in the sea with me,' he said.

He was doing his lifeguard training and was always at the beach.

When Helen came back and told them she'd found a dog that she thought ticked all their boxes, Tula couldn't believe it. As she explained it was a Newfoundland crossed with a German shepherd, the boys' mouths dropped open with excitement.

They'd asked for a big dog and when gentle giant Rocky walked into the meeting pen, they realized they didn't come much bigger. With his thick black fur and amber eyes, he was more bear than dog and the first thing he did was shake his head and slobber flew everywhere.

Tula's first thought was, 'Oh gosh what have we done?' Her second was, they were going to need a bigger car. But any reservations she might have had disappeared the minute she saw her boys' faces light up.

The more they were told about Rocky, the more Tula felt like this match was meant to be. Like Dan, Rocky had had a traumatic few months. He was also struggling with his eating and had lost enough weight that the vet was worried about him. It was as if the pair were kindred spirits.

Seven-year-old Rocky had come into Woodgreen after

his owners couldn't care for him any more while they were building a new home. He'd always lived with another dog but she'd recently died and he wasn't used to being on his own. Depressed and sad, he wasn't eating properly and had lost weight.

For Tula, it was a mixed blessing. On one hand she knew exactly what she needed to do as she'd been doing it with Dan. On the other, did she have the energy and the will to go through all the same stress with someone else?

'He's the coolest thing ever,' smiled Alfie and she could see that he was instantly smitten.

They'd been told Rocky was a big softy who liked to sit on people's laps and Alfie went straight over and stroked him. Rocky came over to everyone for a cuddle – everyone that is except Dan. Tula, as well as Helen and Sue, who were watching nervously on cameras from the office, noticed that Dan seemed hesitant and had hung back.

'Come on Dan, go give Rocky a fuss,' Tula encouraged him.

This dog was really for him and even if everyone else in the family bonded with him, if Dan didn't then she knew they couldn't give him a home.

The handler had left some chopped-up hot dogs in the meeting pen for them to offer Rocky but he'd explained that he probably wasn't going to eat them because he was off his food.

They all took some, determined that the dog was going to

come to them. But the deciding moment came when Dan got up and grabbed a piece. Tula held her breath as he put it in the palm of his hand and held it out to Rocky.

Please go to him, she willed. *Please let this work.*

Rocky padded straight over to him, gave the sausage a cautious sniff then quickly gobbled it up.

They all cheered and as Tula saw the look of pure pride and joy on her youngest son's face, she knew that they'd found the perfect match. Rocky was going to be coming home with them.

Because of Rocky's ongoing medical issues and worries about his weight, it was another three weeks before they could collect him, but the change in Dan was instant. All he talked about was when they were going to be able to bring Rocky home.

The night after they got back from Woodgreen, Tula felt that familiar churning of dread and apprehension as they sat down for dinner as a family. She wondered how long it was going to take this time to coax Dan into eating a few tiny mouthfuls of a chicken dipper. But, much to her amazement, five chicken dippers later, she realized her son didn't need any encouragement. He was so happy and excited to be finally getting a dog that he wasn't feeling anxious or stressed. Every night he made a real effort to eat as he was determined to set a good example for Rocky.

When the vet finally declared Rocky was well enough

to leave Woodgreen, Russell and Tula went to collect him because there was no room for anyone else in the car. The boys stayed at home but they were waiting at the window and as soon as the car pulled up outside the house, Alfie and Dan rushed out to see him. They knew they had to be calm so they didn't scare Rocky but they couldn't hide their joy and excitement. He went straight out into the garden and sprawled out on the grass while they made a big fuss of him.

Rocky arrived with a long list of things he wouldn't do. Before he'd come to Woodgreen, he'd spent six months living outside in a playhouse in the garden so they were told that he was an outdoor dog and would never come inside. They were also told that he refused to eat out of a bowl and were advised to feed him off a Frisbee instead.

On his first night, they all encouraged him to come into the house but Rocky stayed in the garden. The boys sat by his side for hours.

'Come on Rocky,' Dan encouraged him. 'It's nice and cosy inside and you can be with us.'

He wouldn't budge but they left the patio doors open so he could see them inside. When it got to 10 p.m. they tried one last time.

'Rocky please come in,' begged Alfie, desperate for him to come inside before they locked up for the evening.

Much to their delight, this time he got up and wandered into the house. He sprawled out at the bottom of the stairs and promptly fell asleep. From then on, he never stayed outside again.

There were still ongoing concerns about his weight. Rocky still hadn't been eating as much as he should have been when he'd left Woodgreen so the family had been told to monitor him carefully and keep in constant touch. For the first few days, Tula tried to tempt him with all the foods that they'd been told that he liked. She tried chicken with pasta and rice, ham and his favourite type of dog food. They put it on a Frisbee and in a bowl but Rocky wasn't interested in any of it.

They were all getting worried about him, especially Dan.

'I'll help him to eat,' he told Tula. 'And he's going to have his food in a bowl. I think he'll listen to me.'

That night, Dan noticed him sniffing around the barbecued pulled pork that Tula was making for dinner. So he put a little piece of it on the floor to try and tempt him.

'Rocky,' he called. 'Come on, good boy. Come and have some dinner.'

Rocky came over and gobbled the piece of the pork up so Dan dropped another one. Bit by bit, Dan dropped pieces of meat onto the floor, making a trail towards his bowl.

'Ooh look at this Rocky,' Dan encouraged him.

Rocky ate them one by one and when he finally got to the bowl, he ate everything in it. It was the first time that he'd ever eaten from his bowl in the house and the grin of pride on Dan's face is something Tula will never forget.

'Well done boy!' he smiled, giving him a fuss. 'You're so clever.'

From then on, no matter how fussy he was with others, Rocky would always take food from Dan.

Another reason Tula had wanted to get a dog was to encourage Dan to be more confident and independent. One thing he'd always found difficult was communication. If someone spoke to him, he wouldn't make eye contact with them and he would look away. After years of therapy, his speech had improved but he still found it hard to talk to anyone outside his immediate family.

Dan loved taking Rocky for a walk and one day he insisted on taking him into town to get some food for him from the butcher.

'He's your dog so you should go in and ask for the food yourself,' Tula told him when they got to the shop.

She expected him to make the usual excuses or beg her to do it for him. She couldn't believe it when he walked into the shop without any fuss or hesitation. Tula stayed outside with Rocky and watched through the window while Dan chatted to the butcher and told him all about his dog. He pointed to Rocky waiting patiently outside.

'That's not a dog,' laughed the butcher. 'It's a bear.'

Dan came out a few minutes later, proudly clutching a huge bag of lamb bones that Rocky tucked into when they got home.

Before they'd got Rocky, Dan was never interested in going out for a walk. At the time, Tula just thought he was being lazy but looking back, she realized that he hadn't been eating enough so he probably didn't have the energy.

One evening he slowly worked his way through a whole plate of chicken dippers. Tula was stunned when he ate the lot without needing any encouragement.

'I've got to keep strong so I can take Rocky for a walk,' he told her.

He and Alfie proudly walked Rocky along the sea front every day. He was such a distinctive dog that wherever they went, people stopped and chatted to Dan and he'd happily answer their questions about Rocky and what kind of breed he was.

In January 2021, coronavirus rates started to rise and the UK was plunged into another lockdown. Dan was unable to go to school and he was also worried about Tula who worked as a GP's receptionist. His anxiety returned and much to Tula's distress, he stopped eating again. Dan's weight plummeted to three and a half stone and he had to be admitted to hospital. Again, Tula was determined to do anything she could to prevent him from having a feeding tube.

However, this time Dan had something motivating him to get out of hospital: Rocky.

'This is my dog Rocky,' Tula overheard him telling the nurses. 'He's amazing and I miss him so much.'

He showed them all photographs of Rocky on his phone.

In turn, Rocky was also pining for his best friend. When he'd first gone to Woodgreen he'd struggled with a constant upset stomach and when Dan was in hospital, it came back. Tula knew it was because he was stressed and sad that Dan wasn't there.

After Dan had been in hospital for five days, the doctors let Tula take him home for an evening.

'I know you've been missing Rocky so you can come home for a few hours and see him,' she told him.

Dan's face lit up and she knew he couldn't wait to see him.

As soon as he came through the front door, Rocky ran to him.

'I've missed you so much Rocky,' Dan told him, giving him a hug.

He didn't leave Rocky's side for the two hours until Tula had to take him back. In the car on the way back to the hospital, Dan didn't say a word. Tula could see how upset he was to have to leave his best friend again.

'Don't worry,' she told him. 'You'll be home soon.'

Dan arrived back at the ward with a phone full of photographs of Rocky to show the nurses.

His visit home to see his beloved dog had made Dan determined to get out of hospital as quickly as he could. It was such a relief for Tula when he started to eat again.

Finally, after eight days, he had put on enough weight to

be discharged and he was allowed to come home. Dan had missed Rocky so much when he was in hospital, he didn't want to go back in and so he continued eating.

As the months passed, their bond grew even stronger. Dan tripped over in the garden one day and cut his hand open. Normally he would go to Tula for comfort but instead, he ran to Rocky who nuzzled him better.

Rocky's weight was still an on-ongoing worry too. Because they were taking him for several walks a day, he'd started to lose a bit of weight.

Tula could see Dan was concerned. He made sure he filled Rocky's bowl and he'd sit with him while he ate.

'Come on Rocky,' he encouraged him. 'If you don't eat your dinner you won't have enough energy to go for walk with me and Alfie.'

Dan knew that just as Rocky had to eat his food to stay well, he did too. He made sure that he had four small meals a day plus snacks to try and build his own weight up.

Rocky helped him in other ways too. Dan was nervous about going back to school after the long lockdown but Rocky helped give his confidence a boost. He'd always struggled to make friends but his classmates had seen him on TV and they wanted to know all about Rocky. It gave Dan something to talk to them about and he started to enjoy the attention. Rocky even helped him with his schoolwork. He wrote stories about Rocky and he also won a poetry competition for his year group with a poem about his beloved dog.

For Tula, it's such a relief that both Rocky and Dan are on the right path now when it comes to their eating. Rocky is on a raw food diet which has solved his stomach problems and both he and Dan are putting on weight. Occasionally they both have little dips but they always help each other to get back on track. Tula has also got a lot more chilled about Dan's eating. If he doesn't eat occasionally or picks at his food, she tries not to stress and knows that hopefully he will eat more at the next meal.

When their episode of *The Dog House* aired on TV, the family all sat together and watched it with takeaway pizzas. Halfway through the episode, Tula glanced across to Dan and saw that he was tucking into his pizza. He was eating the middle bit while Rocky was enjoying the crust.

'I like pizza because it reminds me of getting Rocky,' he grinned.

For Tula, Rocky is the perfect dog for them. He's given the whole family a new lease of life and has massively lifted their mood. They all take it in turns to walk him, Dan is in charge of his food and Alfie brushes him and has taught him to catch a ball. Russell takes him for walks on the beach and in the rock pools and Alfie swims in the sea with him, which he loves. When Dan is on his PlayStation in his bedroom, Rocky lies in the doorway.

Rocky has brought them all closer and because of him, they spend more time together. He's extremely chilled and sleeps a lot but he's also very funny. He loves going out and when they tell him he's going on a walk, he gets excited and starts running around the house.

Rocky loves going in the car and one afternoon they were walking him back from the beach when they passed a man on his mobile phone in his car. He had his window open and before they could stop him, Rocky was trying to climb in through the open window to get into this man's car. It certainly gave him a shock to have this almost human-sized dog wedged in his window.

The whole family agrees that Rocky has brought a new-found joy to the house and they've even got used to the slobber on the walls and ceiling.

CHAPTER FIVE

Manuel

Luke Chapman walked wearily up the stairs to the first floor flat and turned the key in the door.

'Kath?' he shouted hopefully to his girlfriend. 'Are you still here?'

But it was 8 a.m. and he knew that in all likelihood she would already have set off for work.

Alone in the flat, Luke sat on the sofa and stared into space. He was a paramedic and had just finished a gruelling thirteen-hour nightshift. He was absolutely exhausted but he knew that after what he'd just seen, there was no way he would be able to sleep.

In the last fifteen minutes of his shift, they'd received a call-out to a baby who had gone into cardiac arrest.

Luke and his colleagues had done everything they could but unfortunately by the time they'd arrived, it was already too late. They'd then had to explain to the poor family that their baby hadn't made it. Luke would never ever forget the look of anguish on those parents' faces or hearing the mother's guttural cries. It was just unthinkable what those people were going through.

Now he'd clocked off and had come home, but in his head Luke was still replaying the events of the past hour. Was there more they could have done? What if they'd got there a few minutes earlier? Something that traumatic and distressing didn't just disappear the minute he finished his shift, and he knew an incident like that would stay with him for the rest of his life.

Coming home to an empty house didn't help. He knew that later on he would be going out for his next night shift when Kath would be coming in from work. Sometimes they barely even got the chance to say more than a hello to each other.

Luke thought getting some sleep might help. But when he forced himself to go to bed, he only managed a couple of hours' rest as he couldn't get his mind to switch off. For the rest of the day, Luke tried to keep busy to stop himself from thinking and dwelling on things.

'How was work?' Kath asked him when she got home that night.

There was half an hour before Luke had to go out of the door again.

'Oh – er it was OK,' he told her.

Kath had become an expert at spotting the signs. She could tell something traumatic had happened by his evasive reply and the way he wouldn't make eye contact with her.

She couldn't help but worry about him. Luke wasn't good at talking about his feelings or sharing things that had happened at work with her. She knew it was because he didn't want to upset her and that it came from a good place. However, she could tell that Luke got down sometimes and she was concerned that he didn't have any way to offload. There was the option to get professional help at work if they'd experienced something particularly traumatic, but Luke preferred to try and deal with it himself.

It had always been that way ever since they'd met three years ago at a pub quiz. Kath was there with her family and after a couple of glasses of wine, they'd got chatting. They'd been living together for a year now and were saving up for a house.

By sheer chance, they both worked for the ambulance service – Kath in communications and Luke as a paramedic.

Kath knew how much Luke loved his job but was also aware that sometimes he found it hard to switch off. Paramedics were normally the first at a scene, and he saw people when they were at their worst and most vulnerable. Every day he dealt with panic, upset and trauma and it was hard for him not to be affected.

His shift patterns meant that Luke often worked nights and weekends. One Saturday, Kath had spent the day at her parents' house and had just got back to the flat as Luke got home.

Kath's heart sank when she saw him. He looked broken as he sat on the sofa with his head in his hands.

He was really quiet and she could tell straight away that he wasn't in the mood to talk.

'How was your shift?' she asked him.

'It was all right,' he sighed. 'We were called out to some really poorly people today.'

As soon as he said that, Kath knew that he'd been to something traumatic.

In reality, Luke had been one of the first on the scene at a horrific car crash where several people had died.

He couldn't stop thinking about it but he didn't want to tell Kath. What was the point in upsetting her too?

Kath knew when something wasn't right though. Luke was emotionless and wouldn't answer her questions. For the rest of the evening, he wouldn't sit down and she could see that he was desperately trying to keep himself busy.

When they got into bed, he lay there with a worried look on his face.

'What is it?' asked Kath. 'I can tell that there's something.'

'Oh, something happened at work today and I can't get an image out of my head,' he said.

'Do you want to talk about it?' she asked him, but he shook his head.

Kath had to accept that was the way he dealt with things.

When the pandemic hit the UK in March 2020, Luke had a new kind of situation to deal with. People were fearful of going to hospital and were reluctant to call an ambulance, so his shifts were a lot less busy. When he was called out, he spent a lot of his time reassuring terrified people who thought they had Covid or transferring people who had caught it to hospital.

Luke's biggest fear was catching Covid and bringing it home to Kath who could in turn pass it on to her family.

After every shift he'd come home, put his clothes in the wash and have a shower.

When the whole country went into lockdown, both he and Kath found themselves at home a lot more when they weren't working. They would drag themselves out for a walk but their days off were long and boring.

'I wish we had a dog,' sighed Kath one day.

She thought it would give them a reason to go out and give their walks a sense of purpose.

They'd talked constantly about getting a dog ever since they'd got together. They had both grown up with dogs and their second date had been to a dog rescue shelter. Wherever they went, they would gaze longingly at strangers' dogs and imagine their own.

They weren't allowed pets in their rented flat, but recently they'd got permission from their landlord to look after Luke's mum's dog when she'd gone away on holiday. It had gone well and there was no damage to the flat, so the landlord had said he was happy for them to have a dog of their own.

Luke didn't need any more persuading. Their plan had always been to get a rescue dog so one weekend they went onto the Woodgreen website because it was close by.

'Aw, look at this one,' sighed Kath as she looked through the available dogs.

'I want all of them,' Luke replied.

There were a couple of dogs that had already caught their eye so they filled in an application form. They were delighted when they were contacted to take part in *The Dog House* TV programme, and in November 2020 they went to Woodgreen to meet the staff.

'We're not really fussy about breeds,' Luke told pet advisor Helen. 'But we know what we don't want.'

They weren't keen on smaller dogs like French bull-dogs, pugs or chihuahuas – mainly because Luke was tall and clumsy and he didn't want to risk tripping over and hurting it.

'We'd love a medium-sized dog like a lurcher, a whippet or a King Charles spaniel,' explained Kath.

They didn't mind taking on a nervous dog or one with issues.

'Personality is the most important thing,' said Luke. 'I'd love a cuddly dog that wants to lie on top of you.'

Helen could tell that the main priority for them was having a dog that was really affectionate and tactile. She came up with Manuel, a two-year-old lurcher who looked more like a greyhound.

Manuel had been dumped in a ditch and found by a member of the public who'd heard him whimpering. He'd been discovered cowering under a bush with a mangled leg and had been brought into Woodgreen. Luckily he'd been found in time to save his broken leg and, after an operation, it was healing well.

He was very timid and scared around people. Staff at Woodgreen suspected that he was an ex-coursing dog who'd been abandoned by his owners when he'd broken his leg and wasn't much use to them any more. He didn't know how to play and they thought he'd probably been permanently outside in a yard with lots of other dogs.

They were desperate to find a home for Manuel as he hadn't been treated well in his previous life and they knew that timid dogs like him often took a long time to be rehomed.

Helen only had one concern about the meeting.

'I don't know whether Manuel will find it all too over-whelming,' she said.

However, she knew this dog was the size and look that

would really appeal to Kath and Luke. She just hoped that Manuel would show them how much he wanted to be loved.

She went to tell them the good news that they'd found them a dog.

'He's called Manuel,' said Helen. 'He's a stray that came in to us after he was found abandoned in a ditch with a broken leg.'

Luke was heartbroken to hear what had happened to him.

'How can anyone do that to a dog?' he said.

It was such a sad story and Kath was close to tears. Even though she hadn't even met Manuel yet, she immediately wanted him.

'What made us think this would be a really good match is that he's just so affectionate and loving despite everything that he's been through,' explained Helen. 'He's such a lovely dog.'

Luke and Kath couldn't wait to meet him. Their only fear was that he would reject them.

As soon as Manuel's handler led him into the meeting pen, they both fell instantly in love, but they could see how timid he was.

'He looks so worried,' sighed Luke.

His ears were back, his head was down and his tail was tucked between his legs. His whole demeanor was very sub-missive, as if he was telling them, 'Please don't hurt me.'

Luke and Kath didn't want him to feel overwhelmed, so when his handler let him off the lead, they held back and gave him space while he sniffed his way around the pen. He quickly sniffed out some treats that had been left by the door but, as he nudged the bag with his nose, it dropped to the floor. It was only a gentle thud but it was enough to make Manuel leap from one side of the pen to the other. Luke and Kath could see how jumpy and nervous he was and knew they had to be patient.

They knelt down on the floor so they were more at his level and they waited. They held their breath as, at last, Manuel came cautiously over to them.

Kath couldn't believe it when he jumped up at her for a cuddle.

The first thing she noticed was his big brown Bambi eyes.

'Oh my God his eyes are gorgeous,' she said.

He was so big that when he got on his hind legs he was almost as tall as her.

Even though he was very timid and seemed to be scared of his own shadow, she could tell that he was crying out for affection. She loved the fact that he'd been through so much but he was still prepared to trust people.

Afterwards he walked over to Luke and as he stroked him, Manuel nuzzled into his neck.

Woodgreen staff had told them that Manuel didn't know how to play, but Luke got a couple of balls out. He didn't want to throw them because he knew Manuel's leg was still recovering so he rolled them gently between him and Kath.

He didn't think Manuel would be interested but, much to their surprise, he started bouncing around like a puppy trying to catch the balls.

As soon as he did that, Luke was sold. In his eyes, Manuel was the perfect mix of affectionate and playful that they'd been looking for.

'What we really want to see is him becoming a bit more relaxed,' said Helen, who was watching the meet on a camera from the office.

But they all knew that was going to take time. Past trauma didn't miraculously disappear the minute a dog got a new home. Manuel was obviously comfortable with Luke and Kath and their hopes were lifted when his tail started to wag as they fed him some treats.

Afterwards they took him for a walk and he was really good on the lead. He didn't pull and stayed close to them.

They didn't need to think about it any longer.

'We'll definitely take him,' Luke told Helen.

At the end of November 2020, they drove to Woodgreen to bring Manuel home. His leg was healing nicely and the metal screws had been taken out.

Kath and Luke were so excited as the staff brought him over to them. His demeanor was still very nervous and shy. His head was bowed and his shoulders were down but they could see that his tail was wagging a little bit.

Kath's heart melted at the sight of this timid dog.

'It's as if he's not sure whether he's allowed to get excited or not,' said Luke.

They couldn't wait to get him home, lavish him with love and attention and hopefully bring him out of his shell. On the drive back, Manuel was very quiet and they weren't sure whether it was because he was calm or stressed. He curled up on the back seat with Kath and promptly fell asleep.

When they got back to the flat, they led him through the entrance and up the stairs. But on the second step, Manuel froze.

'Come on boy,' Kath encouraged him, but he wouldn't budge.

'Look, he's shaking like a leaf,' said Luke.

The poor dog was terrified of the stairs.

'I suppose if he's never lived inside a house before, he won't have ever seen stairs,' said Kath.

There was no other option than for Luke to carry him up to the entrance of their flat.

Although he was tall and long, he was still all skin and bone and thankfully he was a lot lighter than Luke had been expecting.

Once they'd got him inside, Manuel nervously sniffed his way around the flat. Because he'd lived outside, they didn't think he'd be used to a dog bed. So instead, they lay an old duvet on the floor of the living room and put lots of toys and treats on it. Manuel gradually sniffed his way around the room and when he finally came to the duvet, they were delighted when he curled up on it. For the next few hours he sat there quietly, his eyes watching them wherever they went.

'Do you think he's OK?' asked Kath, worried.

'He's very quiet but he doesn't seem upset,' replied Luke. 'He's probably getting used to everything.'

That first day he slept a lot and he stayed settled on the duvet overnight.

On the second day, they took him for his first walk. They could tell he was nervous and didn't stray very far from them. As they suspected that he was an ex-coursing dog, they knew they would have to keep him permanently on a lead because if he saw a squirrel or a rabbit, he'd be gone.

As they walked down the pavement, a car approached them. It wasn't going particularly fast but as it passed them, Manuel looked terrified and leapt into the air.

When they got to a puddle on the pavement, he froze and they could see him trembling. He edged around the narrowest patch of grass at the side of the road to avoid the water.

'The poor little guy is so nervous and jumpy,' sighed Luke.

They figured his fear of water had probably been caused by being dumped in a ditch.

As well as short walks, they took him into their large communal garden so he could run around off his lead. When he ran out into the garden one afternoon ahead of her, Kath hadn't noticed a neighbour's cat was sat there.

Manuel's sighthound instincts immediately kicked in and he lunged towards it. The cat managed to jump over the fence back into his own garden but Kath couldn't believe it when Manuel followed. Without much of an effort, he bolted after the terrified cat and leapt over the 6.5-foot fence.

He cleared it without any problem, although the same couldn't be said for Kath who finally managed to scramble over. Thankfully the cat managed to escape but it made them realize they needed to check the garden for cats and squirrels before taking Manuel out.

Having Manuel certainly filled their time. Those first few days with him were spent making sure he had enough to eat and drink and he'd been walked and was happy and comfortable.

Even though Manuel was obviously anxious, he would still let them stroke him. They were desperate for him to let his guard down but they knew it was going to take time to win his trust.

He slept a lot and was still so quiet.

'He hasn't made a single sound since he got here,' sighed Kath.

'Perhaps he's just one of those dogs that doesn't ever bark,' replied Luke.

They both felt the weight of responsibility on their shoulders and because Manuel had been through so much, they were constantly thinking *are we doing this right?*

On his second night with them, Luke and Kath noticed he'd moved off the duvet on the floor and had slept on the sofa instead.

On the third night, he curled up on the sofa again as Kath and Luke went to bed.

Luke was just drifting off to sleep when suddenly he heard a thud. He sat up in bed and peered through the darkness. He could just make out a shape wriggling through their bedroom door and slowly creeping its way across the floor.

It was Manuel commando-crawling his way into their bedroom.

Luke didn't want to turn on the light and frighten him off so he sat and watched as Manuel made himself comfortable on the floor at the foot of their bed.

'What are you doing boy?' he whispered.

But he could tell Manuel was avoiding any eye contact. He curled up and went straight to sleep.

Every night after that, as they soon as they went to bed and turned out the lights, Manuel crept his way into their bedroom. As each night passed, he moved closer and closer to them until one night he jumped up onto the bed and curled up by their feet.

One morning, when he'd been with them two weeks, Kath opened her eyes to find a furry head on the pillow next to her, snuggled in between her and Luke.

'Hello Manuel,' she smiled.

She loved the way he was slowly learning to trust them and he wanted to be near them.

After that, it was amazing how he quickly he transformed. He'd gone from being a timid dog that curled up on the sofa on his own to a dog who liked to lie on top of them in bed and had no sense of their personal space.

One night Kath and Luke decided to have dinner at the table so they could talk to each other for a change, rather than giving all their attention to Manuel. As they put the food on the table and sat down, he wandered over to them with a puzzled expression on his face.

They tucked in and he stared up at them with his amber eyes as if to say, 'Why aren't you sitting with me?' Then, much to their utter amazement, he barked.

Kath almost choked on her food.

'He barked!' she laughed, and Manuel did it again.

It was the first time that they'd heard his voice and it was wonderful.

'Clever boy,' said Luke.

They both rushed over and made a fuss of him, their dog-free dinner plans quickly abandoned. It was reassuring to know that he finally felt comfortable enough with them to be able to use his voice.

From then on, Manuel would bark playfully whenever he wanted their attention.

He was gradually coming out of his shell and he loved

being fussed over. He would come over to one of them, bark and then press his bottom against their leg until they gave in and stroked him.

The first few weeks after they got Manuel, the whole country was plunged into another lockdown. Luke's shifts were crazily busy as Covid cases shot up and the number of call-outs soared. It was non-stop and exhausting.

During one particular night shift, he'd been called out to many Covid patients. People who were in a bad way and were struggling to breathe.

Luke had done his best to reassure them, but it was hard when he was wearing full PPE. He could see the fear in their eyes as they struggled to get air into their lungs. He'd dropped many of them off at hospital but he would never know what happened to them. He ended this shift mentally and physically exhausted.

By the time he got home, Kath had already left for work but when he pushed open the door of the flat, Manuel was there to greet him.

He came running over, wagging his tail, and barking for a stroke. It instantly made Luke smile.

'Hello boy,' he told him.

He sat on the sofa and Manuel instantly jumped up next to him and Luke gave him a fuss.

Rather than sitting there, dwelling on all the distressed Covid patients he'd treated that night, Manuel took his mind off things and instantly helped him de-stress.

Instead of going straight to bed and struggling to sleep, Luke took Manuel out for a walk. Being out in the fresh air, watching Manuel sniff his way around, helped Luke to clear his head and lifted his mood.

When they got back home, he got into bed and Manuel jumped up and snuggled next to him. Having his warm, furry body practically lying on top of him was so comforting and Luke drifted off to sleep.

Mentally and physically, Luke's job took a lot out of him. It was nice to come home to this cuddly dog rather than sitting there alone and dwelling on his own thoughts.

Kath could see the difference that having Manuel had had on Luke too. When he got in from work and saw him, he would perk up straight away and he seemed a lot happier.

Luke's shifts were very anti-social. If he worked a weekend then he would have days off in the week when Kath and everybody else he knew was at work. But having Manuel gave him a purpose and something to do on his free days.

He'd take Manuel for a walk, then they'd go for a coffee at a local café. Afterwards, they'd go to the pet shop and Luke would buy Manuel some new toys, making sure that he sent Kath lots of photos of their adventures. It was much better for Luke's mental health to get out and about and he never felt alone now he'd got Manuel.

When Luke was on nights, Kath loved having Manuel there too. Having him by her side made her feel protected and safe when Luke wasn't there.

At Christmas, they were due to go to Kath's parents but when lockdown rules changed, they had to spend Christmas day on their own. But instead of feeling sorry for themselves, they had a lovely day with Manuel by their sides for company. He made them feel like a little family and it was special to share his first Christmas just with him.

He kept them going through the long winter lockdown. Instead of sitting in the house, Manuel encouraged them to go out for a walk in the fresh air and they kept themselves busy with him. Luke was always pleased to get home from a long, stressful shift at work and see him run to the door.

Manuel has changed Kath and Luke's life and they've transformed his too. To see him go from being a really anxious dog with his head down and his tail between his legs to a confident, happy and playful dog has made them so happy. In fact, they can't imagine life without him.

CHAPTER SIX

Coco

Imagine your child being perfectly healthy one minute and the next, unconscious and fighting for her life in hospital.

Up until two years ago, Rebecca Hillings' daughter Kiya was a lively eight-year old. High energy, full of fun and with a wicked sense of humour, she was always busy and loved dancing, gymnastics, drama, horse riding and cheerleading. She was Rebecca's only child and Rebecca and her husband, Kiya's stepdad Ian, doted on her.

Then one morning in March 2019, everything changed. Kiya was sent home from school with a bad headache. Rebecca suffered from migraines and she worried that her daughter was getting them too.

She got Kiya settled on the sofa, gave her some painkillers and was sure she'd be back to her happy self after a bit of rest. But over the next few hours, Kiya's condition deteriorated and by that evening she couldn't speak or even move.

Terrified, Rebecca called 999 and she was rushed to hospital. As she watched her daughter, screaming in pain and being sick in the back of the ambulance, she felt scared and helpless.

As soon as they got to the hospital, Kiya started having seizures. It was the most horrifying thing Rebecca had ever seen.

'Somebody do something,' she yelled to the nurses. 'She needs help.'

Over the next twelve hours, much to Rebecca's distress, Kiya kept fitting. Unsure what was wrong with her, the doctors put her to sleep and she ended up in the high-dependency unit. At first they thought it was an inflammation of the brain called encephalitis or meningitis; however, tests ruled out both of those conditions.

After sixteen hours, Kiya woke up and over the next few days she recovered well. The doctors knew from scans that there was something going on in her brain but they didn't know what. After eight days, she was finally allowed to go home.

To start with, much to Rebecca's relief, Kiya seemed completely normal. She went back to school and did all the things that she loved. However, she started to have more seizures every couple of months. Each time it happened, she had to be rushed to hospital so doctors could administer a powerful drug that was the only way of stopping them.

The doctors were convinced there was something else causing the seizures other than epilepsy so, as the months passed, Kiya had endless tests. Rebecca had also started to notice a few other worrying signs.

Sometimes Kiya repeated things that she'd already told them and her arms and legs often hurt. She was outside in the garden one night skipping with her friend and the next day her arm was so sore, she couldn't move it.

'I think I've pulled a muscle on the skipping rope Mummy,' she told Rebecca, but Rebecca knew instinctively it was something more serious.

The seizures were getting more and more frequent but the barrage of tests didn't find anything conclusive.

A painful lumber puncture was followed by a muscle biopsy in January 2020, where doctors took part of Kiya's thigh to examine. In March, Rebecca was due to see the paediatric neurologist to get the results. After a long year of worrying and not knowing what was wrong with her little girl, she desperately wanted answers but at the same time she was dreading what they might have found.

But when the whole country was plunged into lockdown because of Covid, they weren't allowed to go into hospital. Instead, their appointment became a phone call.

Rebecca nervously put the neurologist on loudspeaker and listened.

'I'm so sorry to have to tell you this over the phone but the biopsy showed that Kiya has mitochondrial disease.'

Rebecca and Ian had never heard of it. The consultant explained that it was a group of rare conditions that meant Kiya's muscles didn't function properly because they weren't getting the energy they needed to keep going.

Rebecca had so many questions. At least now they knew what it was, they could start to treat it.

'I'm afraid there is no treatment or cure,' the neurologist told them gently. 'It's terminal.'

She explained that Kiya had a severe strain of the disease that had come on very suddenly.

'I'm afraid Kiya's condition will gradually deteriorate as her muscles shut down.'

It was the worst news that any parent could hear and, sat there in her living room, Rebecca struggled to take it in. In a matter of minutes, her entire world had been ripped apart. Rebecca thought of her energetic, confident, chatty little girl who she could hear playing happily upstairs and it was unthinkable.

She felt like she'd been punched in the gut. After the initial shock, she sobbed and sobbed until she had no tears left.

'What are we going to tell Kiya?' she cried to Ian.

'We have to tell her the truth,' he replied.

Rebecca knew they had to be honest but she also knew that there were some things her daughter didn't need to know right now.

Rebecca took Kiya's hand and gently explained to her about the disease.

'What does it mean Mummy?' she asked.

It broke her heart but Rebecca had to tell her.

'It means that you're always going to be poorly,' she said. 'You're not going to get better I'm afraid.'

She explained that she would get very tired and her legs would eventually stop working and she would need a wheelchair.

At first Kiya didn't say much. Rebecca could see it was taking a while for it to sink in.

Later on that day, the tears finally came.

'Why me?' she sobbed. 'Why have I got poorly?'

'I don't know darling,' Rebecca sighed. 'I know it's so hard for you but whatever happens, we'll deal with it. We'll take each day as it comes. Ian and I are here for you and there are lots of doctors who want to help you.'

Rebecca was doing her best to put on a brave face and stay strong for her daughter but inside she was falling apart.

The disease was genetic and further tests showed that Rebecca was also a carrier. She had a much milder form and without Kiya being diagnosed, it was unlikely that she would ever have realized.

The tests also showed that she and Kiya were the only two people in the world with this particular strain of mitochondrial disease.

'I'm afraid it means we can't give you any definitive answers,' the neurologist told her. 'We're learning from Kiya.'

Much to Rebecca's distress, Kiya deteriorated quickly. Her energy levels plummeted and she got tired very easily. She would be walking along when her legs would suddenly give way and she'd collapse. It broke Rebecca's heart to see her struggling but Kiya would just pick herself up off the floor as best she could and carry on.

A few weeks after her diagnosis, Rebecca gave up her job as a cleaner to become Kiya's full-time carer. After a few months, Kiya couldn't walk very far so they had to start using a wheelchair when they went out, but she never complained. She was also getting very weak and they were struggling to get enough food down her. Because of the disease, her muscles needed as many calories as they could to keep them working. If she didn't eat enough, there was a risk her whole body would start to shut down. So in September 2020 she had a feeding tube fitted.

Kiya's diagnosis had completely turned their world upside down. They had to move because their house couldn't be adapted for a wheelchair and Rebecca struggled to get Kiya up and down the stairs if Ian was at work. They moved to a new house with the aim of converting the garage into a bedroom and wet room for Kiya. Because she got so tired, she could only manage three hours at school a day.

Rebecca was determined to stay upbeat and strong for Kiya and not cry in front of her, but she would get very down. It was devastating to watch her daughter deteriorate at the hands of this cruel disease, knowing that there was nothing she could do. Some nights she'd cry herself to sleep and she struggled to even talk about it. Ian would try and get her to open up about how she was feeling but she would just break down.

One afternoon Kiya was sleeping. She'd had a stomach bug so she was being fed through a feeding pump that she was attached to for seven hours a day. It meant she couldn't move around and Rebecca had to help her do everything.

She was so fed up and in pain, but she finally fell asleep, so Rebecca came downstairs for a break.

It was a sunny day and the back door was open. As Rebecca sat in the kitchen with a cup of tea, she could hear the sounds of a sports day going on at the local primary school.

She could hear the children laughing and the parents cheering and her heart broke for her little girl. A year ago she'd been at Kiya's sports day, cheering her on from the sidelines. Rebecca remembered her determined face as she'd won the skipping race. She'd been so proud of her as her teacher had presented her with a medal.

Now she was lying in bed, sleepy and in pain, and she barely had the energy to walk upstairs. It was so unfair. Rebecca sat there and cried for everything the disease had taken away from her daughter.

Kiya was so strong but she had her down days too. One day she knew her friends were performing in a drama show that she was supposed to be in and she burst into tears.

'I just want to be normal and do all the things I used to do,' she sobbed.

Rebecca knew it was so hard for Kiya because she still remembered being well and all the things she used to enjoy. She'd always been really confident and outgoing and she loved being on stage and performing.

'I know darling,' Rebecca told her. 'It's not fair but this is our new normal and we can still do lots of fun things.'

She tried to make sure that Kiya had lots to look forward to, since so many of the things she loved doing simply weren't possible any more.

Rebecca tried to always have something planned to cheer Kiya up. She loved swimming and she was weightless in the water so they would try and take her to a pool, if she felt up to it. Sometimes they'd book a night away to help keep her spirits up or her friends would come for a sleepover. A charity called the Lily Foundation, who helped raise awareness of mitochondrial disease, treated them to a weekend at Center Parcs.

Rebecca knew there was one thing that would cheer Kiya up. She loved animals and ever since she was a toddler, she had always wanted a dog. They already had two cats, Mister and Daizy and a bearded dragon lizard called Sid. Rebecca had always worried about how the cats – especially Mister who was very old – would cope with a dog around. So they'd decided to wait until he'd died before they got one as she didn't want to upset him.

But now Rebecca was trying to make every day count with Kiya and she knew that getting a dog would cheer her up and help boost her morale when she was feeling low. Rebecca would do anything to bring a smile to her daughter's face.

'Let's just go for it,' Ian agreed.

Rebecca and Kiya loved curling up and watching *The Dog House* together, and because of the show, Kiya desperately wanted a rescue dog.

Woodgreen was an hour away from their home in Lincolnshire so Rebecca registered with them and filled out an online application form. At the bottom, she saw a message that said if you're interested in appearing on the show, tick this box.

She ticked it, but didn't think any more about it until they had a phone call a few days later. She explained what Kiya was going through and Woodgreen said they'd like to help.

When Rebecca told Kiya what was happening, she was so excited. Her two big dreams in life were to get a dog and go on TV, so they were both hopefully about to come true.

'Oh I might get a puppy,' she grinned.

'I think it's unlikely you'll get a puppy darling but we'll definitely see if we can get a younger dog,' Rebecca told her.

She knew puppies didn't come into rescue centres very often and she didn't want to get Kiya's hopes up.

Rebecca and Ian knew they were doing the right thing as for the next few weeks, that was all Kiya talked about and just the thought of getting a dog had put a smile on her face.

On the day they went to Woodgreen, she bought a cuddly toy dog with her.

Rebecca told pet advisor Lizzie about Kiya's rare medical condition and how they wanted a dog to help cheer her up and make her feel better.

'I think for Kiya to have a dog to look after, to have someone that loves her as much as she loves it, would be the ultimate happiness for her,' she told her.

When it came to breeds, they explained they wanted something small, cute and fluffy, like a Pomeranian or a chihuahua, that would be gentle around Kiya. She was desperate for a female dog as she wanted to buy it a pink lead and a shiny collar.

Lizzie came up with an idea but she was worried that it would be too much for Rebecca and Ian to cope with. Recently the first ever litter of cockapoo puppies had been born at Woodgreen and there were three puppies still available. The breed – which was a mixture of a cocker spaniel and a poodle – had become extremely popular. They were boisterous, active and needed to be kept busy.

Lizzie decided to get their opinion first.

'I know you wanted a younger dog but would you ever consider a puppy?' she asked them.

When Lizzie told them about the litter of cockapoos, Kiya screamed and Rebecca cried.

She couldn't believe it. Kiya had always wanted a puppy and Rebecca's favourite breed of dog was a cockapoo. It was everything they'd ever wanted and she was overcome with emotion.

Meeting three puppies was Kiya's dream but they were worried they wouldn't be able to choose one of them to take home.

The puppies were only six weeks old and still hadn't had their jabs, so they were brought into the meeting pen in a carrier. Kiya squealed with delight when she saw the parcel of puppies.

When they opened up the carrier, all three puppies ran straight to her. Kiya lay down on the floor and they leapt all over her. Rebecca couldn't stop smiling as she watched her daughter giggling and laughing as she played with these adorable pups. It had been months since she'd seen her this happy.

Rebecca knew Kiya wanted a girl and two out of the three were females – a black one and a chocolate brown one.

Rebecca watched the black one tear around. She was very manic and Rebecca was worried that she would pull out Kiya's feeding tube. The brown one was playful but she seemed a lot gentler and she had a placid, calm side too. She snuggled into Kiya's lap and licked her face.

'I'd like this one,' smiled Kiya.

They decided to call her Coco because of her chocolate-coloured fur.

They had to wait until Coco was eight weeks old until they could bring her home. Every single day Kiya asked when they were getting her.

In November 2020, a week before Kiya's tenth birthday, Rebecca drove to Woodgreen to collect the puppy. She didn't tell Kiya as she wanted it to be a surprise.

When she got in from school, Rebecca was sat on the sofa with Coco on her lap. Kiya said hello and didn't notice the puppy at first, but when she finally spotted her, her face froze in amazement and she went over to her.

'Happy early birthday darling,' Rebecca told her.

She was so excited. 'Coco's my best ever present,' she declared.

The other part of Kiya's present was accessories for Coco – a turquoise collar with pink flowers all over it and a pink glittery heart name tag and a black and gold bed with her name on it.

The reality of having such a young puppy began to hit home. Like all puppies, Coco did play-biting and would nip Rebecca and Ian's fingers and toes, yet thankfully she was always very gentle with Kiya. Their original plan had been for Coco to sleep with Kiya but while they were house-training her, she slept in an open crate next to Rebecca and Ian's bed. During this time, they were getting up four times a night to take her out to the garden. It was like having a newborn baby. They were exhausted and started to wonder whether they'd done the right thing.

Rebecca's main worry had been how the cats would react to the new member of the family, but these fears were unfounded. Daizy and Coco quickly became friends and Mister tolerated her and learnt to keep his distance. Coco loved Sid the bearded dragon and followed him around. She would nudge him gently as if she was trying to get him to play with her, but she left him alone when he showed no interest.

However, as soon as they saw how much Kiya adored her they knew they had made the right decision. During the long days at home, Coco provided non-stop entertainment. One day Kiya was crawling around on the floor and Coco was following her.

'Come on Coco,' she laughed.

As she giggled away, it hit Rebecca how lovely it was to hear her daughter properly laughing again.

Kiya loved playing with Coco and, depending on her energy levels, Rebecca would always try and include her. If she was feeling good, they would have a kickabout with Coco in the garden. Coco loved her ball, although she wasn't very good at dropping it so they needed two. If Kiya wasn't feeling well then she would sit in her wheelchair and throw the ball to her instead.

If Kiya was well enough to go to school, she missed Coco terribly. But the greeting she got when she came home made it worthwhile. Rebecca had put a stairgate in the hallway so if the front door was open, Coco couldn't get out. When Kiya came in the door, Coco would jump up at the stairgate and make noises that almost made it sound like she was talking.

'It's like she's singing and dancing Mum,' Kiya laughed.

Coco never failed to make her smile, but was calm when she needed to be too.

One afternoon Kiya wasn't feeling well so she was resting in bed. When Rebecca came in to check on her, she was worried to find her sobbing.

'What is it darling?' she asked.

'Please can you close the window Mum,' she asked her.

She explained that she could hear the neighbour's children playing outside.

'It's making me so sad cos I can't do that any more.'

Rebecca felt her pain. It was just so unfair. She sat on the bed with her and held her while she cried.

As she gave her a hug, she heard the gentle tapping of tiny paws on the floor and Coco ran into the bedroom. She leapt up on the bed and gently licked the tears from Kiya's face. Before long, Kiya was giggling as Coco drowned her in so many kisses, she had to come up for breath.

Rebecca was constantly worried that Coco would accidentally pull the feeding tube out of Kiya's nostril as she was so energetic. But it's as if she knew it was part of Kiya and she was extremely gentle as she licked carefully around her nose.

Coco didn't like Kiya getting upset and if she ever cried, she was there in seconds. Rebecca was astounded. For such a young puppy, she was so intuitive and it was if she had a sixth sense that told her when someone was upset. When Kiya was crying she never did it for long because she didn't want to upset Coco.

Coco always knew what Kiya needed. If she was upset, she was there instantly to either lick away her tears or just cuddle up with her on her bed or the sofa. And the times when Kiya was feeling OK, Coco was boisterous, full of fun and ready to play and make her laugh.

Rebecca had convinced herself that they were getting a dog for Kiya so she hadn't thought about the benefits that Coco would have for her too.

She wasn't the sort of person who would go out for a walk for no reason but having Coco meant that she had to take her out.

There was a gate at the bottom of their garden with a bridge that led over to a riverbank and Rebecca started to take Coco there every day.

One afternoon she went out when Ian was back from work. After being in the house caring for Kiya all day, she felt her shoulders relax as she strolled down the river with Coco who was enjoying sniffing her way along. It was the first time that she'd been out all day and it was a chance for her to have some space, breathe and clear her head.

Sometimes she'd meet her mum Evelyn and her dog – an elderly Yorkipoo called Roxie – who Coco absolutely loved. Being outside and walking with Coco was such a boost for her mental health and she looked forward to it.

She hadn't realized how lonely she'd been until they got Coco. Now she had a constant companion. Coco was like her shadow – she wouldn't leave her side and would follow her around the house. They had put her dog bed downstairs in the living room but Coco spent every night sleeping on top of the bed in between Rebecca and Ian.

The days would sometimes feel long for Rebecca. With Ian at work and Kiya sleeping a lot, she would sit downstairs on her own. Those were the worst times as that was when Rebecca's mind would wander. She would remember how her daughter used to be and worry about the future and all it held.

Rebecca always tried her best not to get upset in front of her daughter. Kiya had caught her crying a few times but she'd always made up an excuse as to why she was upset.

Rebecca tried to distract herself from her thoughts one day by logging onto Facebook. She was friends with lots of Kiya's friends' mums from school and their feeds were full of photographs of them enjoying the holidays with their children and having days out doing all the fun things that Kiya could no longer do.

Rebecca sat and cried. A few seconds later she heard the pitter patter of tiny paws on the floor and a chocolate-brown head appeared at her feet.

'Hello Coco,' smiled Rebecca, and before she knew what was happening, Coco had leapt up onto her lap. She then proceeded to lick her tears away exactly like she did with Kiya.

It made Rebecca feel bad because she knew how much Coco hated seeing any of them upset.

Even when Rebecca was at her lowest, Coco would make her smile. Both she and Kiya had sessions with a counsellor but for Rebecca, Coco was the best therapy.

Her bonkers behaviour made them all smile. Kiya's favourite was what they called 'the zoomies', which was when Coco would have a mad twenty minutes and just tear round the house for no apparent reason.

'She's completely crazy,' smiled Ian, and it would leave them all howling with laughter.

She was such a funny, silly dog and it helped them all to have that distraction. She made Rebecca laugh and instantly feel better and able to face the afternoon without having to sneak off into the bathroom to cry.

At night, when Kiya was in bed, Coco would cuddle up with Rebecca on the sofa. She loved her tickles and she'd lie on her back with her legs in the air in a most unladylike fashion while Rebecca rubbed her belly.

'You are adorable,' she smiled.

Now Rebecca can't imagine life without Coco. In her opinion, Coco has saved them. She has brought their family so much joy and made things a bit brighter for everyone. They're going through the most horrendous thing that any parent could ever experience, yet they can't help but be happy around Coco. They all adore her and Rebecca knows she's been so good for Kiya. She's always there for her to cheer her up when she's down, to comfort her, lick her tears away and to make her laugh.

Rebecca and her family knows that whatever the future holds for them, they will get through it with Coco by their side.

Emma Colclough, Dog Carer

Emma Colclough stared at the clock. It only felt like a few seconds since she had last checked the time but the day was dragging. She was literally counting down the hours until she could leave the office and go home.

That night, as she walked in through the front door of the house she'd just brought with her boyfriend Theo her heart felt heavy.

'Good day?' Theo asked her.

'No not really,' she sighed. 'I just don't think I can do it any more.'

Ever since she was a teenager, Emma had wanted to be a lawyer. She'd studied law at college for two years before she'd done a law degree at Lincoln University. That was followed by a Legal Practice Course (LPC) and then a Master's in Law in Cambridge.

After six long years of studying, she'd finally got a coveted job as a solicitor at a law firm in Cambridge. It was what Emma had worked hard for, she was earning a good salary and her parents were so proud of what she'd achieved.

But the truth was, Emma wasn't enjoying it. She was stuck behind a computer all day, she didn't get to meet many clients face to face and the work was dull and endless. When her alarm went off every morning, her stomach would sink with dread and she felt a permanent sense of gloom. She would spend all day watching the clock, willing the time to pass.

'I honestly can't wait until the weekend,' she told Theo. 'It's the only thing that keeps me going.'

Every other weekend, Emma worked as a dog carer at Woodgreen looking after the dogs in the kennels. She'd started there to earn a bit of pocket money while she studied for her Masters. She loved every minute of being with the dogs and she knew she couldn't give it up when she got her job as a solicitor.

She'd grown up with pet cats but she had always been obsessed by dogs. Her parents, Sally and Mick, had a photograph of her trying to train her cousin's Border collies when she was nine. She'd persevered until she'd managed to teach them to sit as well as a few tricks.

When she'd started at Woodgreen, first on reception and

then as a dog carer, it didn't feel like work. Her job was to feed the dogs, clean their kennels, train them, walk them, give them a bath if they needed one and just spend time hanging out with them. Emma loved the fact that she built up such a good relationship with the dogs and she was their mum for the time that they were there. She'd see them at their worst when they came in and then she'd make sure that by the time they left, they were at their best.

A stray could come in on a morning and it would be growling at her and absolutely terrified. Then by the end of the day, it would be bouncing all over her because she had managed to win its trust. It was amazing to help an animal transform and Emma had so much to do that the days went by so quickly. She found it hard to let go on a Sunday and the dogs were constantly on her mind all week at work. She'd keep in touch with her Woodgreen colleagues and text them to see how they were doing.

After a long, dull week at the law firm, Emma couldn't wait to get back there again the following weekend.

As she walked into the kennels on Saturday, one of her colleagues stopped her.

'Guess what?' she said. 'Magic's found a new home.'

'Oh that's brilliant,' smiled Emma.

Magic was a lurcher and he was one of the first dogs Emma had helped to train. He was a stray who'd come into a rescue and been rehomed, but his new owners had given him up as he had so many behavioural problems. He would lunge and bark at other dogs and Emma knew if they didn't try and sort his issues out then it would be difficult for him to find another new home.

She had spent weeks finding out what motivated Magic and working out how she could help him. She loved the challenge of training a dog – it was like a puzzle that she needed to solve. Emma was learning along with him too.

When Magic saw another dog, she'd offer him a distraction. He could go and bark at the other dog and get upset or he could come to her, get a bit more space and have a nice treat. Slowly, he'd learnt to walk away from what was upsetting him and after a couple of months, he wasn't bothered by other dogs any more.

Later that day, Emma went to say goodbye to him as he left for his new home. She had a lump in her throat as she watched him trot away with his new owner, his tail wagging. As they were walking off towards the car park, his little head turned round and he gave her one last look that made her eyes fill with tears.

She had loved helping Magic and he'd left Woodgreen as a totally different, much happier dog.

It had only taken Magic a couple of months to change his behavior but for some dogs, it took years. It was so satisfying for Emma to know that she had played a part in that and she knew she would never get that same feeling from being a solicitor.

With the arrival of their rescue dog Buddy and baby daughter Willow, Tony and Joanne finally have the family they always dreamed of.

Lorraine and her son Oliver have found their perfect match in West Highland terrier Norman.

Obi at the local cricket field, where Mike enjoys taking him for a walk several times a day.

Above: Sue with her late husband Ritt, and their family of five dogs (*left to right*): Nanuq, Lara, Reef, Mush and Squidgy.

Left: Dan with his best friend Rocky. They have helped each other through some hard times.

Paramedic Luke with Manuel, who helps him switch off from the stresses and strains of his job.

Coco the cockapoo is always there for cuddles with eleven-year-old Kiya.

Woodgreen dog carer Emma has loved every minute of training her terrified chihuahua, Nellie.

Lisa on the day she collected Sherlock from Woodgreen and took him back to his forever home.

Louise and her mum Angela love exploring new places with Nya.

The Job family now can't imagine life without energetic Jack Russell, Rocco.

Right: Six-year-old Oscar calls rescue dog Ludo his little brother and loves snuggling up with him.

Below: Woodgreen pet advisor Helen and her husband Alex with their rescue pups Amber and Susie, who helped them get over their previous dog's death.

Left: David loves the time he spends having adventures with Pebbles.

Below: Lola the puppy came into Sharron's life when she needed her the most and now she's always by her side.

Poppy the rescue dog is the perfect companion for Father Miles and encourages him to get out and about each day.

It was then that Emma knew she couldn't do law any more. She knew in her heart that it wasn't something that she could see herself doing for the next forty years, whereas working with the dogs at Woodgreen was her passion.

However, her and Theo had just bought a house and she couldn't leave without another job to go to. There were no full-time vacancies at Woodgreen and so she waited nearly a year for a dog carer job to come up. Emma applied and thankfully she got it.

Now she had to hand her notice in at the law firm and break the news to her parents. It was a scary conversation for Emma to have with them and she didn't honestly know how they were going to respond. They were so proud of her becoming a solicitor and she was worried about disappointing them.

'I'm leaving law and I've got a full-time job working with the dogs at Woodgreen,' she told them.

They looked shocked at first.

'Are you sure, after all those years of studying?' her mum, Sally, asked.

'I've never been so sure of anything in my life,' Emma replied. 'Law doesn't make me happy but working at Wood-green does.'

After they'd had some time to get used to the idea, thankfully they were behind her.

'As long as you're happy that's the most important thing,' her dad, Mick, said.

It meant a lot to Emma to know she had their support.

She didn't feel any regrets as she handed her notice in at the law firm a few days later. It was the happiest day of her life and as she walked out of the office, Emma wanted to dance down the street. A huge weight had been lifted.

Emma couldn't believe it was finally happening and she knew Woodgreen was where she was meant to be.

She started there straight away after working her notice. It was such a relief to be doing a job that she enjoyed. She couldn't wait to get into work every day to see the dogs and it was such a different feeling.

Now she was working full time at Woodgreen, Emma knew that she wanted to finally get a dog of her own. But first, she decided to foster. It was a great way of working out what kind of dog would fit best into their lives.

Staff were able to pick which dogs they wanted to foster.

Some staff temporarily fostered a dog just so they could see how they were in a home environment, which was useful when they were writing their assessments. Emma tried to pick dogs who just really needed the chance to get out of kennels.

She loved big dogs and her and Theo's dream had always been to have a Rottweiler. When an old Rottweiler called Inca came into Woodgreen, Emma immediately offered to foster him. The poor old boy had lots of medical issues and they soon realized there wasn't enough room for a large dog in their small house with its tiny garden.

'OK maybe we need to go smaller,' Emma suggested.

So Inca was followed by a series of Jack Russells. Emma wasn't looking at them as prospective pets so she fostered whichever dogs needed it.

They'd just decided to have a break from fostering for a while when a colleague called her over to tell her about a stray puppy that had just come in.

'She's only twelve weeks old and too young to be left in a kennel,' she said. 'I wondered if you'd mind fostering her?'

Emma thought about it for a second. She didn't have any other dogs living with her at the minute so she had the space and she couldn't turn away a puppy in need.

'That's fine,' she said. 'I'll take her.'

She went to go and collect her from the welcome centre where new animals were dropped off. The warden was stood there holding a blanket and curled up inside it was the tiniest dog that Emma had ever seen in her life.

'This is Nellie,' she told her. 'She's a chihuahua cross.'

She was completely emaciated, covered in fleas, shivering and shaking with fear. The warden told her that she'd been abandoned in Cambridge and had been living rough for the past few weeks.

'Oh my goodness,' sighed Emma. 'It's a wonder she survived.'

Most of the rats in the city must have been bigger than this little thing that could fit into the palm of her hand and only weighed one kilogram.

As Emma took her in her arms, Nellie looked up at her with huge, fearful brown eyes.

'Let's get you home,' she told her.

As Emma drove Nellie home, she could see she was terrified of the world. Any noise or movement left her shaking with fear.

She hadn't told Theo that she was bringing her home – just in case he said no! He was already at home when she walked through the door with Nellie in her arms.

'Look who I've agreed to foster,' she told him.

'Oh wow she's tiny,' he gasped.

But Nellie took one look at Theo and let out a high-pitched scream.

Emma had never heard a dog scream like that before and it was horrific. It sounded just like a young child in distress.

Nellie was terrified of Theo and Emma had to take her into a separate room to calm her down. It soon became apparent that Nellie's biggest fears were men and black bin bags, which they guessed were related to the circumstances in which she'd been dumped.

Emma spent the next few days feeding her four times a day, desperately trying to build her strength up. She was very unsettled as she didn't know what a house was so everything scared her, from the noise the washing machine made to the front doorbell ringing.

She was glued to Emma's side and refused to go near Theo which really upset him.

'What can I do to make her less scared of me?' he asked.

'Just ignore her,' Emma told him. 'Give her time and space and she'll get to know you in her own time.'

She knew that if you pushed dogs that were really nervous then they'd become even more withdrawn. Theo did exactly what she said and he left her to it and occasionally threw some treats in Nellie's direction.

Slowly, as the weeks passed, Nellie began to go nearer and nearer to Theo and gradually started to get used to him. Once she became more comfortable with him, Emma decided to leave her at home one day with Theo while she went out to work.

She spent all day wondering how they'd got on and worrying whether Nellie would be OK without her. She couldn't wait to get home and see her.

But when Emma came in that night, the house was silent. She walked into the living room to find Theo and Nellie curled up on the sofa together, fast asleep.

From then on, Nellie was absolutely besotted by Theo and followed him around everywhere.

Emma knew she was getting very attached to Nellie too. They'd had her for four weeks by now and the time was coming up for her to be rehomed. One evening, Nellie came and jumped up on Emma's lap. Instead of facing out like most dogs did, she faced her. She looked up at Emma with those huge brown eyes and Emma instantly knew that they couldn't give her back. Nellie was their dog.

'Theo I can't do it,' she told him. 'I can't give her up. I want to keep her.'

Luckily he felt the same way. From wanting a massive bruiser of a dog, Emma couldn't believe that he would end up with the world's tiniest chihuahua.

But when Emma went into work the next day and told the rehoming section her plans, they dropped a bombshell.

Nellie had already been advertised on the website as up for adoption the previous day and, in a matter of hours, someone had already reserved her. Even though she worked at Woodgreen, Emma couldn't be given priority over a member of the public if they had made their decision first.

A few days later they arranged to come to Woodgreen to meet her. Emma was terrified. Nellie was so cute and special and the thought of having to give her up to someone else and say goodbye to her was heartbreaking.

As Emma had been fostering Nellie for the past few weeks, she had to come to the meeting to talk to the prospective adoptees about her.

Emma knew she had to keep it professional but she felt sick.

'Nellie's very nervous when she meets new people,' she explained to them. 'So rather than going straight over to her, it's best to leave her alone and give her some space so she comes over to you.'

When Emma brought Nellie in, she hid behind her and wouldn't come out. The couple were trying to reach around and grab her so they could pick her up and Nellie was getting more and more scared.

'She's so timid,' they said at the end of the meet. 'We don't think she's for us.'

For Emma, it was such a relief.

'You're staying home with Mum,' she told Nellie, giving her a cuddle.

They'd come so close to losing her, they couldn't wait to give her a permanent home.

Nellie was still a very nervous dog but Emma wanted to help her face her fears and get over them rather than swooping in and rescuing her every time.

At first it was very stressful taking her out. People thought small dogs were cute and they would often approach Nellie but if she saw a man, she'd be petrified and scream. They had a large country park near their house so they would try and take her for a walk at quieter times. If she did see a man and got scared, Emma would take her away and reassure her.

Nellie was the first dog Emma had ever had in her life and she was teaching her so much.

'I'm becoming an accidental expert on training nervous dogs,' she told Theo, but it was true.

Everything she was learning with Nellie she could use with other dogs at work.

Nellie was so sacred of everything that progress was very slow. But Emma knew that they just had to be patient and give her constant reassurance.

Whenever they went on a walk and saw a man approaching, Emma would gradually lead Nellie closer to them to see how she would cope.

It has taken nearly two years to start seeing the changes but now Emma has helped Nellie to become a different dog. She's playful, loving and has really come out of her shell. Nellie used to bark shrilly at men, absolutely terrified of them but she's finally got over her fears and when new people come over to her, she loves to meet them. If she sees a man now she isn't as afraid but she still looks to Emma for reassurance.

Emma has been working at Woodgreen full time for just over two years and she's still learning every day. Leaving law was the best decision that she ever made and she has no regrets. Being able to help a dog like Nellie at one of the worst moments of their life is such a gift and there's no other job she'd rather do.

CHAPTER SEVEN

Trinity

Louise Thompson had a plan. She was working in Spain as a singer for the summer, performing in music bars and nightclubs. She was doing what she loved and enjoying the sunshine.

Her ultimate goal was to travel, so at the end of the season in October her plan was to head to New Zealand for a couple of years. It had always been her dream and she couldn't wait.

In her late twenties, she was older than most of the other entertainment staff. So while they frittered their wages away in a few days on bar crawls, she put as much of hers away as she could.

Louise had been in Spain for three months when she was having a drink with some friends in a bar one evening after work. It had been a good night and she was enjoying herself – until a woman walked in. Louise could tell by the way that she had staggered into the bar that she'd been drinking and Louise had an uneasy feeling as she charged over to their table.

'Let's go,' she whispered to her English friend and house-mate Marica, keen to get out of there as quickly as possible and avoid any drama.

But it was too late. As Louise got up to leave, the woman started shouting all kinds of insults at her, including racial slurs. Feeling horrified but not wanting to make a scene, she grabbed her handbag and headed for the door.

'I can't believe she's saying those hideous things,' fumed Marica.

'Let's just get out of here,' replied Louise.

She couldn't get away quickly enough, as she could just tell this woman was trying to provoke a reaction and Louise didn't want to give her the satisfaction. With her heart pounding, she and Marica headed out to the street.

Louise breathed a sigh of relief as they walked out into the warm evening air. It was upsetting to be verbally abused like that but this stranger had had her moment and caused a scene like she'd wanted to. Louise just wanted to get home and forget about it.

A few seconds later, she screamed in surprise as someone came up behind her and violently yanked her hair. She heard her neck crack and the shock made her stumble backwards and she landed on her bottom on the street. Unbeknown to them, this woman had followed them out of the bar.

Too stunned to speak, Louise managed to get to her feet and she and Marica went to walk away when the woman launched her second attack. She ran up behind Louise and grabbed her neck. Louise could feel her hands tightening around her throat and she was terrified.

Marica desperately tried to pull the woman off her friend but Louise went into fight-or-flight mode and eventually, with a surge of adrenalin, she managed to loosen this woman's hands and push her away. Coughing and gasping for air, Louise and Marica ran home to their apartment, not daring to look behind them. They didn't say a word until they got inside and locked the door.

'What the hell just happened?' gasped Marica. 'What on earth was her problem?'

Louise realized she was shaking and her neck had started to ache.

The pair of them sat there in silence for a while, both too shocked to talk.

It was the early hours of the morning by now and starting to get light. Louise was exhausted after working all night so she went to bed. But as she lay there, her mind was racing, thinking about what had just happened to her.

She must have eventually nodded off but when she woke

up a few hours later, her neck was throbbing and she could barely move it.

'You should report it to the police,' Marica told her. 'She racially abused you and she's injured you too.'

Louise went to the police station and told them what had happened. She only spoke basic Spanish but with the help of Google translate, she managed to get by.

They advised her to go and get examined at the local hospital. An X-ray showed that thankfully there was nothing broken, although her neck was badly bruised. She was sent away with strong painkillers and a neck brace. She also had a huge bruise on her lower back from where she'd fallen and hit the floor.

Later that day, Louise went back to the police station and gave them a statement. She took a local friend with her who helped translate. Much to her relief, they took it seriously and were going to find the woman and question her.

Louise went back to her apartment, still shaken and in pain. She didn't feel safe any more. It was only a small town and she knew she was going to be constantly worried that she was going to see this woman again. What if the police went to talk to her and she came back to find her?

Louise was in too much pain to get on stage and sing that night. She spent the next day holed up in her apartment, too scared to go out. She called her mum Angela, who she was very close to. Angela was horrified when she told her what had happened the previous night.

'Please come home,' she told her, clearly worried.

Louise put on a brave face and tried to brush it off.

'I'll be fine Mum,' she reassured her. 'I'm not going to let her ruin my plans.'

But she knew she couldn't stay in that town any more. Two days after the attack, Louise packed her bags and got a train to Benidorm. Her friend Anthony lived there and it was a busy resort so Louise knew she had a good chance of picking up singing work. It was only when she got to the safety of his apartment that she allowed herself to break down. All the fear and shock of the past couple of days came tumbling out.

'I'm sorry,' she sobbed to him. 'I don't know why I'm letting it get to me.'

'I'm not surprised,' he replied, concerned. 'You've been racially and physically attacked.'

Because of the ongoing police investigation, Louise didn't want to leave the country and she was determined to get on with things. She knew she could only stay with Anthony temporarily as there wasn't room in his apartment. However, it was mid-season and everywhere was booked up so she struggled to find accommodation. She moved between hotel rooms and expensive short-term lets which were quickly eating into her savings.

As the days passed, her neck started to heal; however, she still felt very jumpy and anxious.

Louise was on stage one night singing and, as she looked

out into the crowd, she thought she saw the woman who had attacked her.

Oh no, she thought. *She's here.*

Her heart was racing and her whole body was shaking. Even though eventually Louise realized that her mind was playing tricks with her and it wasn't her, she knew she would constantly be looking over her shoulder. She'd started to feel very alone and was increasingly worried about money.

That night when she got back, she called Angela.

'Mum I can't handle it,' she told her, crying down the phone. 'I don't think I can do this any more.'

'Please come home,' her mum begged her.

With her plan to spend the summer singing in Spain abandoned, Louise headed back to Croydon.

She'd been trying to be brave but the more time she had to digest it, the more she realized that the attack had actually been quite frightening and it had left her traumatized.

Angela was waiting for her at the airport and as Louise sank into her mum's arms, she was overcome with relief. For the first time in three weeks, she finally felt safe.

As soon as she got home, Louise's plans fell apart. She knew she wasn't going to make it to New Zealand and she shut herself off from the world and didn't want to leave the house. She'd suffered from anxiety and depression after her dad had died twelve years ago but she'd gradually come through it and got her confidence back. Now Louise felt she was back in that dark place again.

Angela was desperately worried about her and did her best to persuade her to leave the house.

'Come to the supermarket with me,' she asked her one day.

Louise reluctantly agreed but as soon as they walked into the shop, it was overwhelming. She could feel her blood pressure rising and her whole body was burning up like she was on fire. The bright lights hurt her eyes and every noise felt like it had been amplified.

'I need to go home now,' she mumbled to her mum. 'I can't do this.'

She stopped going out at all and her world got smaller and smaller. Occasionally Angela would persuade her to come outside to the garden for a barbecue but Louise would eat and go straight back inside. On really bad days, she wouldn't leave her bedroom.

Increasingly desperate, Angela came up with ways to entice her out. She'd make her a cup of coffee and leave it on the kitchen table so that Louise would have to leave her room.

Even though she was close to her mum, Louise didn't want to talk about what had happened. She couldn't. She didn't want to do anything. She didn't want to sing any more or see friends.

Every day she thought about the attack, reliving it over and over again in her mind.

In bed one night, as she closed her eyes, she was back on that cobbled street. She felt herself falling to the floor as her hair was yanked back and then she felt hands around her neck, gripping tighter and tighter, squeezing the life out of her.

Louise turned the light on, gasping for breath, convinced that she was back there on that warm summer's night in Spain.

Plagued by constant flashbacks and panic attacks, her anxiety was sky-high and she didn't trust anyone any more. The days just slipped by in a blur. Some days Louise wouldn't do anything except watch TV. Angela would get home from work and find her in the same position that she'd left her in that morning.

Louise tried to snap herself out of it and keep busy. She decided to buy a sewing machine and try her hand at making clothes. She thought that doing something creative might help take her mind off things.

But when she cut out a pattern for a dress and got out her sewing machine, she just sat there for ages, staring at it, unable to muster up the energy or the enthusiasm. Eventually Louise screwed the pattern up in frustration and threw it into the bin.

She'd lost her drive and passion for anything and she felt numb.

It wasn't a good place to be and Louise hated it but she couldn't see a way to get out of this state of mind. What was she doing with her life? She'd had so many plans and ambitions to travel the world and now here she was, unable to leave the house.

After a year of emails and phone calls to the Spanish police, Louise discovered that the legal proceedings weren't going to go any further. She was devastated but it was then that she decided she couldn't carry on like this any more. She couldn't waste any more of her life dwelling on what had happened; somehow she had to try and force herself to move on from it.

She went to see her GP and explained what had happened in Spain and how she was feeling.

'You've got post-traumatic stress disorder,' he told her.

Louise was shocked.

'That's ridiculous, I can't have that,' she told him.

She wasn't a soldier who had fought in a war.

He explained that the flashbacks, depression and panic attacks were all symptoms of PTSD triggered by a traumatic event, which, in Louise's case, was her attack.

He prescribed her antidepressants and some one-to-one cognitive behavioural therapy (CBT) sessions. It was a relief for Louise to know that there was a reason as to why she felt like she did.

The weekly CBT sessions would give her a focus and would force her to leave the house but she was dreading it. Going out had become such a big thing and she needed time to prepare herself mentally.

The morning of her first session, she was terrified. The clinic was only a twenty-minute walk away but as she closed the front door behind her and stepped out onto the street, it felt like the hardest thing that she had ever done.

Her head was spinning and she felt hot and panicked but she repeated the same thing over and over in her head.

Just breathe, take your time, you can do this.

As she walked, Louise realized that nothing was happening to her and she was OK.

Somehow she managed to get herself there and back which gave her a huge sense of achievement. Every week it didn't get any easier but Louise would make herself go to the sessions. On other days, she would go for a drive. It was a way of getting out and about and having a change of scenery and she felt safe in the confines of her car.

Little by little, she started to grow in confidence. Another idea was also floating around in Louise's mind.

'Shall we get a dog?' she suggested to her mum.

They'd always wanted one but the timing had never been right. Angela was a teacher and was out working every day and Louise had expected to be travelling the world for the next two years. Now due to the pandemic, Angela was working from home and Louise had abandoned her travel plans. As far as getting a dog went, it was an ideal time.

Angela still worried about her daughter. She had heard dogs were good therapy and she was secretly hoping that getting one would help Louise get out and about more.

They signed up with several animal charities and rescues around the country, including Woodgreen which they remembered from watching the first series of *The Dog House*. They knew it was a big place so they thought there would be more chance of getting a dog through them.

In August 2020 an email arrived inviting them to apply to be on the programme. They talked it through and decided to go for it.

Louise desperately wanted a dog but this would be their first experience of having one and she had a few concerns. She was scared at the thought of having to take it out several times a day for a walk and not being able to go at her own pace. On her bad days was she going to neglect it? She didn't want to get a dog and then let it down.

On the way to Woodgreen, she confided in Angela.

'It's a big responsibility Mum,' she sighed. 'What if we can't cope?'

'We'll manage it together,' Angela reassured her.

At Woodgreen, the pair described their ideal dog to pet advisor Helen.

'We'd like a dog who knows when it's time to get excited and then when it's time to light the incense and relax,' Louise told her.

She explained what she'd been through over the past year since the attack.

'I love the idea of going for a walk but I always feel really anxious and I don't end up going because I think it's more effort than it's worth,' Louise explained. 'I think a dog will help me feel a lot more confident and secure.'

The staff immediately came up with five-month-old lurcher puppy Trinity. She'd been brought in because of her jumping up and mouthing – which is where dogs use their mouths to explore people and objects without actually biting down. It's common behaviour for puppies but it had scared her owner's young children. Since she'd come into Woodgreen, the staff had worked hard to redirect Trinity's bouncy, exuberant energy. Personality-wise they thought she would be an ideal match for Angela and Louise because she was outgoing and sociable and loved meeting other dogs and people.

Neither Angela nor Louise knew what a lurcher looked like but they were both excited and nervous as they headed to the meeting pen.

When Trinity ran through the door, she ran straight over to Louise, jumped up at her and gave her a lick – and had a good chew on her shoelaces. Louise warmed to her straight away and she loved her sassiness and confidence.

Angela immediately fell in love with this cute, energetic pup but Louise was still feeling anxious about whether she would be able to cope. You couldn't help but fall in love with a puppy and she knew her mum was very much sold on Trinity so she had to be the voice of reason.

So many thoughts were racing through her mind as they

took Trinity for a walk around the grounds at Woodgreen. Could they really do this? Was Trinity too strong? If she ran off, would Louise be able to chase her?

Louise had fallen for her too but she was trying to be realistic. Her confidence was so low and she was still battling her mental health and struggling to find her feet. Would this energetic puppy who was into anything and everything be too much?

But she was so cute and playful and Louise loved her trusting nature. So she made a decision.

'Let's just go for it,' she smiled. 'It's a new chapter.'

It all happened very quickly. Within a week they were back at Woodgreen to pick Trinity up. They'd decided to give her a new name to reflect her strong personality.

Louise had chosen Nyabinghi – Nya or Ny-Ny for short – based on one of her favourite folk tales about an African queen who was betrayed by her husband and possessed other women and led them to greatness. She'd always loved this story of a strong woman scorned and thought it really suited their willful new puppy.

When Angela opened the door of their basement flat, Nya tore in. She ran around the whole place, sniffing everything in sight. She wasn't nervous or hesitant at all.

They thought they'd put away everything that she could possibly find but a few seconds later, she came trotting out with one of Louise's sewing patterns in her mouth, followed by some cardboard which she immediately ripped to shreds.

'I think we need to buy her some toys – and quickly,' laughed Angela.

They took her to the garden and let her off the lead and she ran madly around and around in circles.

The following day they took Nya for her first walk to the local park. Instead of feeling anxious about going out, Louise was excited.

There was no question about whether she could leave the house or not, because there wasn't any time to mentally prepare herself or dwell on it. Nya needed a walk and they had to take her.

Louise had tried to go out on walks in the past but she found it difficult to walk round aimlessly on her own without any purpose. She would always start to feel panicked and she would end up coming home. Now they had Nya, it gave Louise a reason to go out and she wasn't thinking about herself or her anxieties.

Angela came too and as they walked to the park, Louise didn't feel panicked or unsafe. She was too focused on Nya and her needs. Was she OK? How would they know when she needed a wee? Did she know the difference between the road and the pavement?

As she proudly held Nya's lead, she felt confident because they had her with them. They'd bought her a long lead so she could go off and explore without them worrying that she was going to run away. They watched her and laughed as she sniffed patches of grass and ran in and out of the bushes, excitedly exploring every inch of her new neighbourhood.

For Angela, it was a huge relief to see her daughter outside enjoying the fresh air with a smile on her face and she instantly knew that getting a dog had been the right decision.

Louise looked forward to walking Nya every day and she started researching different places they could take her to. She quickly learnt that she was very sociable and loved meeting other dogs.

Nya was so friendly and on Louise's first walk alone with her, she bounded over to say hello to a group of dogs and their owners. For the past few months, Louise had made any excuse that she could to avoid seeing and speaking to people. Most days she had only spoken to her mum.

But as Nya dashed over to them excitedly and tugged the lead, Louise had no other choice but to follow. As she walked over to the group, she felt her stomach churning with nerves. But the other dog walkers were very friendly and made her feel instantly at ease.

'Oh I absolutely adore lurchers,' smiled one woman. 'What a beautiful girl. How old is she?'

Louise answered her questions and told her about the show and Woodgreen. Dogs gave them a common ground and something for her to talk to them about.

Even a few weeks ago, chatting to a group of complete strangers would have been Louise's worst nightmare. But she enjoyed talking to them and she came away smiling. Nya had pushed her well and truly out of her comfort zone but it had given her confidence a real boost. It was nice to know that she could go out on her own and speak to people. She hadn't panicked; in fact, it had felt OK.

Wherever they went on a walk, Louise always ended up talking to someone. She soon discovered people loved lurchers and Nya was so bubbly and friendly, she made it easy for her to go over to people and have a chat.

Louise still had her bad times. One night as she lay there wide awake, she could feel the anxiety rising in her chest. She pulled the duvet up around her head but she felt too stressed to sleep.

Then suddenly she felt something warm and wet nudging her nose as a little face appeared next to her.

'Hello girl,' she whispered.

Louise hadn't been making any noise but it was as if Nya knew that she was awake and sensed that she needed her.

Nya stared at her with her soulful amber eyes and licked her cheek, and then she waited.

'Come on then,' smiled Louise, patting her bed.

Nya immediately jumped up and settled down next to her. It was so comforting having a warm body to curl up with and it instantly settled Louise.

The bad days still happened but they were fewer and

fewer and because of Nya, they were short-lived. She was so affectionate and offered immediate comfort if Louise wanted a cuddle. Or if she needed cheering up, Nya would run madly round the room in circles and Louise couldn't help but laugh.

'You're so silly,' she smiled.

It was as if Nya always knew exactly what she needed.

Angela noticed the change in Louise too. Instead of bottling things up, she was a lot more open about her mental health. They'd walk Nya and it would give them time and space to chat about how she was feeling.

Having Nya encouraged Louise to make plans. She loved to find new walks for them and she wanted to take her places and go exploring.

She discovered that she enjoyed being outside in nature and the fresh air really gave her a boost. In the school holidays when Angela was off work they took Nya on her first holiday to the Brecon Beacons. They went on long walks every day and Nya loved it as she tore up hills and splashed through rivers with a little backpack on her back filled with her treats, water and a towel in case she got wet. There were waterfalls and beautiful scenery everywhere. Louise loved it because she could see that Nya was enjoying it and in turn, that made her happy.

By the beginning of the second lockdown, Louise felt strong enough to start working again. She bought some equipment to create a studio at home and began working as a session singer. It meant that she could be there for Nya during the day.

In July 2021, Louise had her first gig since she had last sung in Spain. It had been over two years since she'd performed on stage and she was so nervous.

She'd bought a beautiful sequined dress and, as she stepped on stage and heard the cheers of the crowd, she felt a rush of adrenalin and confidence. For the next two hours, Louise finally felt like her old self. It was the most amazing feeling being able to sing live in front of people again. Thanks to Nya, her spark was slowly coming back.

With Nya by her side, Louise had finally moved on from what happened in Spain. Sometimes she still had dreams that she was back there but it didn't affect her as much as it used to. It wasn't holding her back any more and she could live her life again. Having Nya boosted her confidence and helped her to move on. She looked forward to getting up in the morning because with Nya she never knew what each day was going to hold – Nya would always make her laugh or do something silly.

For Angela, after years of worry it's a relief for her to have her daughter back to her happy, chatty self and she knows a lot of that is thanks to Nya. Although they had both worried that getting a dog would feel like a lot of responsibility, now they can't imagine life without Nya.

CHAPTER EIGHT

Shane

Lisa Green quickly opened the wardrobe in her spare room and shuddered. Shame burned inside her as she saw all the things crammed into it that she had bought over the past year – clothes with their price tags still on that didn't even fit her, designer make-up and perfume that she'd never used and – the most ridiculous of all – three brand-new dinner services still in their boxes.

Why did I even buy them? Lisa thought to herself.

They each served twelve people and she lived on her own.

Lisa was so angry with herself. She'd wasted so much money on all these things she didn't need, but she couldn't stop herself going on these spending sprees.

It had all started when Lisa's dad Harry had passed away

suddenly. After having circulation problems in his leg for years, he'd had an operation to amputate it from the knee down.

'The operation went very well,' the nurse at the hospital had told her when she'd called to see how he was doing. 'He has come round now and has already sat up in bed.'

Lisa had gone to see him and he'd been laughing and joking around until suddenly he'd gone very pale and started pulling on his drip. She knew something was seriously wrong.

'Somebody please help him!' Lisa screamed, as she lunged for the emergency button next to his bed.

Medical staff had come running but it was too late. Her dad had had a massive heart attack and died right in front of her.

The shock of that had left Lisa feeling numb with grief. With four older brothers, she'd always been a daddy's girl. Whenever she'd felt down, her dad had taken her shopping or bought her something to try and cheer her up. That had been his way of fixing things for her so after he passed away, Lisa went shopping for herself, in an attempt to make herself feel better.

Shopping was a quick fix. She loved the thrill of buying something new and carrying a crisp paper bag with tissue paper in it.

But when Lisa got home, the initial rush of excitement would disappear and she would sit and cry. The overwhelming sense of grief was still there and all the shopping in the world wasn't going to change it.

But Lisa couldn't stop herself. She kept on spending and was so ashamed that she wouldn't take anything back. Instead, she'd shove it the spare room wardrobe. In her mind, if she couldn't see it, it didn't exist.

She was spending money that she didn't have and she was getting more and more into debt. Over the past few years, she'd taken out countless loans and maxed out her credit cards to the limit. Lisa was working full time at a construction company but as soon as she got paid, her wages would go straight out again and she was living off her overdraft.

Things had gradually got worse and now she couldn't even afford the minimum payment every month on all her loans and credit cards. Every time her mobile rang, she was too scared to answer it because she knew it would be the bank or the loan companies demanding money.

Lisa knew she couldn't live like this any longer. She hadn't told any of her friends or family what had happened, and the shame was eating away at her.

'I can't go on like this,' she tearfully told the woman behind the desk at the debt management company. 'I need help.'

Lisa had been in denial for so long, she didn't actually know how much she owed in total. She sat there, terrified, as this stranger worked it out.

'You have £35,000 of debt,' she told her bluntly and Lisa burst into tears.

It was a terrifying amount and Lisa felt like she had nothing to show for it. Just a few wardrobes stuffed full of items that she didn't need.

It was daunting but Lisa was determined to pay off every last penny. She didn't want to declare herself bankrupt as she didn't want to risk losing her house.

She was put on a debt-management programme and she got a second job in a pub where she worked five shifts a week. Half her wages automatically went to paying off her debts.

She was exhausted from doing two jobs, but it kept her away from the shops. Finally, after seven long years, she'd paid everything off.

It felt like a new start. Lisa would always miss her dad, but her grief and sadness didn't feel as all-consuming.

Then a few months later, suddenly Lisa's world was shattered again. Her mum was diagnosed with ovarian cancer. Devastatingly, it had already spread to her lungs.

'I'm sorry but there's nothing more we can do,' the consultant told Lisa. 'Take her home and spend some time together.'

She'd only been given a week to live. Lisa moved in with her. They got a hospital bed in the living room and Lisa slept by her side every night.

It was heartbreaking but Lisa found an inner strength that she didn't know she had. Her dad had died so suddenly and shockingly that there had been no time to prepare. The thought of losing her mum as well was horrendous, but at least they had time to be together and say the things they wanted to say.

Lisa was holding her mum's hand when she passed away three months later.

After losing both her parents, Lisa felt very alone. She'd been single for years but this was a sadness and an emptiness that she'd never felt before.

'I think I'm going to get a dog,' she told her colleagues at the pub where she still worked in the evenings.

Lisa had had a dog when she was growing up – a Labrador-Alsatian cross called Oscar whom she'd loved.

One of the regulars overheard her talking and said, 'You can have mine if you want.'

He explained that he'd got a seven-year-old Weimaraner called Doofa Dog. Lisa laughed when she heard his name.

'I've got a new job and I'm going to be working away a lot,' he told her. 'I can't leave him for that long so I was going to start looking for new home for him.'

'I'll have a think about it,' she told him.

Lisa arranged to go round and meet Doofa the following evening. When she saw him, she couldn't believe her eyes.

'He's beautiful,' she gasped.

He was a gorgeous silver colour and had distinctive amber eyes. Lisa loved big dogs and Doofa was seven and a half stone and the size of a Shetland pony.

'He's big but he's really loveable,' the man reassured her.

'Why don't you take him for a couple of weeks and see how you get on?'

Lisa agreed. She'd only had him for a day when she decided this dog was never leaving her.

Doofa was a real character. The first night she brought him home, she sat on the sofa. Doofa jumped up next to her and plonked himself firmly down on her knee.

Having seven stone of dog sat on her lap wasn't exactly comfortable but it made Lisa smile. He wriggled his bottom which she quickly realized meant he wanted her to tickle his back.

'You're a great big softie, aren't you?' she told him.

Within a few days, Doofa had got her wrapped around his great big paws.

She enjoyed taking him for walks and they'd spend their evenings snuggled up on the couch together. People called Weimaraners Velcro dogs and Lisa could see why. Doofa wanted to be close to her all the time and wherever she went, he was there too.

A few months later, she noticed that Doofa kept pawing at a little freckle on her neck.

'What is it boy?' she asked him. 'What have you found?'

Lisa had first noticed it when her mum was dying but she'd been so caught up with caring for her that she hadn't thought any more about it. But now Doofa had pawed at it, it made her look at it more closely in the mirror. It had started to itch a bit and bleed occasionally and, looking at it now, it seemed to have changed shape and got larger so it looked more like a mole.

Lisa's GP referred her to the hospital where they did a biopsy. A few days later she received a letter asking her to come in for the results.

'I'm afraid it's a malignant melanoma,' the consultant told her.

Lisa was completely floored. Not once had she really thought it was going to be cancer.

She had surgery to remove the mole and they took out some of the lymph nodes in her neck too. Luckily it hadn't spread anywhere else, which Lisa liked to think was thanks to Doofa.

Sadly, there was more heartache to come when a few short months later, Lisa's older brother Derek died suddenly from heart failure. Again, having Doofa by her side brought Lisa so much comfort.

She'd had Doofa for four years when one day Lisa couldn't find him anywhere in the house. She eventually found him outside in the garden, hunched over and crying in pain. She took one look at his swollen stomach and she knew exactly what it was.

She knew that Weimaraners were particularly prone to a dangerous condition called bloat, where their stomach fills with gas, food or fluid and twists. She rushed him to the vet but it was too late.

'I'm sorry but it's too far gone and because of his age, I don't think he'd survive the operation,' the vet told her. 'It's kinder to put him to sleep.'

Less than an hour after she'd found him the garden, Lisa held Doofa in her arms as he died.

She went home, bereft. Doofa had been such a big presence that the house felt cold and empty and it didn't feel like a home any more.

Lisa knew that eventually she would get another dog, but her grief felt too raw at first. Instead, she threw herself into her new job managing a bar and a sports club.

So many customers brought their dogs with them and Lisa would fawn over them. She knew all their names and she'd buy treats and bring them into work for them.

'You must have a dog,' one of the customers told her one day as she fussed over her Labrador.

'I did,' said Lisa sadly. 'But he passed away.'

'By the looks of it, I think you need to get yourself another one,' the woman told her.

Lisa knew she was right but she didn't know where to start. She wanted a rescue dog but she knew that if she went to a rescue centre, she'd want to give every single dog there a home.

When she came across an advertisement for *The Dog House*, it seemed like the perfect solution. Lisa didn't know how she would ever pick one dog to take home, but this way someone would help her narrow it down and make the decision for her.

In August 2020, a year after Doofa had died, Lisa went to Woodgreen.

'I definitely want a big dog who's very loving,' she told pet advisor Helen. 'But apart from that I'm not bothered by age, breed or if they've got any medical issues.'

'You're my dream rehomer,' Helen told her.

Lisa was certain she wasn't a little fluffy dog type of person. Being on her own, she felt safer with a large dog. When she took them for walks, she felt protected and more confident.

But although she wanted a big dog, she didn't want another Weimaraner as it would be too painful and she knew she could never replace Doofa.

Helen was determined to find the perfect match.

'I get the impression Lisa's been through a lot in the past and I think she'd empathize with a dog who'd had a difficult background,' said Helen, as she searched through the available dogs.

Her colleague Wendy immediately suggested a three-year-old American bulldog cross called Shane.

'He's a big bruiser but he's really lovely,' she told her.

Shane's notes said that he was friendly, sociable and loved to sit and watch the world go by. He loved cuddles and to sit on people's laps and give them all the kisses in the world.

Most dogs were at Woodgreen for less than a month before they were rehomed. Shane had been there for ninety days and his handlers were starting to give up hope. Larger dogs were more difficult to rehome. When people saw their size and strength they assumed they were dangerous. This couldn't have been further from the truth for Shane, who was a big softy.

Helen told Lisa about him.

'We have found one dog who we all feel ticks all the boxes. He's called Shane and he's an American bulldog cross,' she said. 'He's a big chunky monkey but a really soppy boy.'

She explained that he'd come from a home where they had two other large-breed dogs.

'The other two dogs were kept inside but Shane lived outside,' Helen told her.

'That's mean,' gasped Lisa.

Her heart went out to this poor dog who she knew must have felt so rejected. As a result of this, Shane was cautious of both new situations and new people and was also anxious around other dogs. Lisa wasn't put off by that and couldn't wait to meet him.

As soon as Shane walked into the meeting pen, Lisa couldn't help but smile. He had one of those faces that made him look like a grumpy old man.

Helen had already warned her that Shane was going to be worried meeting someone new and when his handler left the pen, he rushed over to the door. He put his paws on the glass and stood up on his hind legs looking for her.

'What's up beautiful?' Lisa asked him.

She was determined not to go over to him. If he was feeling anxious, Lisa wanted him to come over to her in his own time when he felt ready. But it was hard playing it cool when she just wanted this dog to love her like she already loved him.

Lisa waved some toys to see if that encouraged Shane to come to her.

'What's this?' she asked, giving them a shake. But Shane walked straight past her, completely disinterested.

She had tried to be patient but, after a while, Lisa started to worry. She would be so mortified and upset if Shane refused to have anything to do with her.

'What's up pup?' she asked him in one final bid to attract his attention.

Finally, after waiting for what felt like an eternity, Shane came cautiously over to her. Even though he was a big dog, she could tell he was timid and submissive. He lay straight on the ground and showed her his belly, which Lisa knew was a sign of fear.

'It's OK boy, I'm not going to hurt you,' she reassured him, making a fuss of him.

She spent the next few minutes talking to him and stroking him and was rewarded with lots of licks and kisses.

'You're a big soft lad, aren't you?' she laughed.

Lisa knew that he'd finally dropped his guard when he came and sat on her lap so she could scratch his back – just like Doofa used to do.

'Go home and have a think about it and see whether you think Shane would fit into your life,' Helen told her.

But Lisa had already made her mind up. She knew she could give Shane a good life and she was prepared to put the effort in with him. He could come to her house and live like a king and she was determined to make him feel loved. Like her, he'd had rough times but she was sure they could make each other happy.

'I definitely want to give him a home,' she told Helen, and three weeks later, Lisa went to pick him up from Woodgreen.

Lisa had already decided that she wanted to change his name.

'I don't want to be stood in the park shouting Shane,' she told her friend Agar. 'It sounds like I'm calling for my boy-friend not my dog!'

'What about Sherlock?' he suggested, and she loved it.

Lisa was so excited to bring Sherlock home. As soon as he walked into the house, she let him sniff everywhere and have a run around the garden.

When she went upstairs to the toilet, Lisa didn't realize Sherlock had followed her until she found him sat outside the bathroom door.

'Hello sunshine,' she smiled. 'Let's go downstairs and I'll get you something to eat.'

But as Lisa walked down the stairs, Sherlock stood on the top step, looked down and froze.

'Come on pup,' she encouraged him but he refused to budge.

That was the moment Lisa discovered that Sherlock was petrified of stairs. She could see that he was shaking with fear and drool was streaming out of his mouth.

Something had obviously happened in his previous home that had caused some sort of trauma.

'Come on Sherlock,' she urged.

Over the next few hours, Lisa tried everything, from gently coaxing him downstairs to going down herself and ignoring him, but he still wouldn't budge. There was no way she could carry him. He was only five stone but he was a big, solid boy and Lisa had an old elbow injury that meant she couldn't lift anything heavy.

Lisa eventually called Woodgreen for advice and they gave her a few tips. She tried cooking some bacon and chicken to tempt him down but he remained frozen on the top step and was too terrified to move.

After ten hours, Lisa knew there was nothing more she could do so she took Sherlock into her bedroom and got him settled for the night.

She covered the floor with puppy pads and brought him up some food and water. He happily ate and then settled down on her bed.

The next day, she tried another few times to coax him down the stairs but with no success.

On the third day, Lisa contacted an animal behaviourist and asked her to come round.

'I've never seen a dog this scared before,' she sighed, as she saw Sherlock looking from the top step.

She suggested two things that Lisa could do.

'You could phone your vet and ask them to sedate Sherlock and then help you carry him downstairs,' she said. 'Or you could get someone to throw a blanket over his head and then quickly carry him down.'

The blanket option felt like the quickest and less stressful for Sherlock, but Lisa was unsure who to ask. She didn't know many people who were strong enough to quickly carry a five-stone bulldog down a steep staircase.

The answer presented itself later that night when her brother Alan called her on his way home from work.

'I just wondered how you were getting on with the new dog?' he asked.

'Well actually I've got a favour to ask you,' Lisa told him.

She explained that for the past three days Sherlock had been stuck upstairs.

'Why didn't you call me before?' he told her. 'I'll come round now.'

Half an hour later, the mission was accomplished and a shocked-looking Sherlock was finally downstairs. He had weed all over Lisa's brother but he looked so happy as he ran straight outside into the back garden.

From then on, Lisa put a stairgate up and Sherlock never went near the stairs again. It had been a stressful start to their relationship, and it had made Lisa worry whether she'd made the right decision. What else was Sherlock going to be scared of?

Lisa knew all she could do was lavish him with love, make him feel like part of the family and hopefully he would feel less anxious.

One night she sat on the couch watching TV. Lisa knew it was only early days and probably way too soon for an anxious dog like Sherlock to have built a bond with her.

But, much to her amazement, Sherlock ran into the room and jumped up onto the sofa next to her.

'Hello sunshine,' she smiled.

He curled up beside her and Lisa put her arm around him. After a year without having a dog in her life, it felt amazing. She found being close to a big dog was so comforting and it instantly brought her peace.

As she stroked Sherlock's white fur, she could see that he was enjoying their cuddle too. She couldn't believe that he was prepared to trust her so soon into their relationship.

She could see that all he wanted was an owner who loved him and who would let him live in the house and cuddle up with him on the couch. Lisa was prepared to do all of that and more. Without a dog in the house she had always been lonely but now Sherlock was here it was like she was part of a family again.

Even though he was a timid and anxious dog, Lisa felt protected by him. If anything moved outside the house, he'd be straight up at the window barking. Lisa had warned friends that were coming over.

'I've left a bowl of treats on the doorstep,' she told them. 'As soon as I let you in, you give him one, and then he'll know you're his pal.'

If anybody else was in the house besides her, Sherlock would walk over to Lisa and sit on her feet as if he was protecting her.

So far Sherlock had only run around in the garden and Lisa was worried about taking him for a walk in public spaces. Woodgreen had warned her that Sherlock was very reactive towards other dogs. If he saw another dog then he would get very scared and agitated and lunge at them.

The staff had given her advice about how to handle it and try and divert his attention away from the other dogs.

Lisa had decided to walk him very early in the morning or late at night so there wouldn't be many people about and to take him to quiet places.

For their first walk, she took him out very early one morning. They were walking along the pavement and Lisa's heart sank when she saw a small, yappy dog on the other side of the road. It was too late to distract Sherlock with a treat, as she knew he'd already seen it.

He didn't bark but as soon as he saw the dog, he tried

to leap towards it. Lisa pulled on his harness. Sherlock was strong but she managed to hold him back.

'It's OK boy,' she soothed as they turned and walked away.

He was very agitated and Lisa could tell that it came from a place of fear, but this behaviour could easily be misinterpreted as aggression.

He was the one who had been hurt in the past, so he wanted to get in first and scare the other dog before they scared him. Her heart went out to this misunderstood dog.

Lisa was committed to helping Sherlock through his issues whilst he helped her with hers. After everything she'd been through, Lisa still had moments of intense grief.

She missed her parents and her brother desperately and thought about them every day. One evening she was watching a film about dads and daughters and Lisa found herself welling up with tears.

She thought about all the lovely things her dad had done for her over the years. She remembered when she'd moved into her first flat and he'd done up the bathroom as a surprise. He knew money was tight and one day she came home to find her dad had done a food shop for her and the fridge and the cupboards were full. When she felt the loss of her family, it helped so much to have Sherlock there.

'I miss dad,' she told him.

Having somebody there to hug when she was feeling low

brought her so much comfort. Stroking his soft white fur always worked like magic. It calmed Lisa down and relaxed her.

She always felt a lot more balanced when she had a dog. When those hard moments happened, Lisa would cuddle up to Sherlock instead of feeling the need to go out and spend money.

As the months passed, he really started to come out of his shell.

After a lot of sadness in her life, he brought Lisa a lot of joy and he was always making her laugh. Whenever she took him out in the car, he refused to get in the back seat. One morning she opened the front passenger side for him.

He jumped in but then he quickly moved across to the driver's seat.

'You OK there darling?' she asked him.

Sherlock looked so funny sat behind the steering wheel as if he were ready to drive. He did that every time he got in the car and he'd give Lisa a weary look as if he was really put out that she made him move.

With Sherlock around, her house felt like a home again. Lisa liked finishing work knowing that he was waiting for her at home. She pulled up one night and he was sat in the living room window, lying on an ottoman. As soon as he saw her car pull up in the driveway, he shot to the front door. Rather than coming home to an empty, dark house, Lisa was greeted with kisses and licks and a floor covered with dog toys. It was lovely having someone who was so pleased to see you they bounced all over the sofas with excitement.

From the second she walked in the house, Lisa could barely move because Sherlock was always there by her side. He was her comfort and having him felt like a void had been filled. Lisa was fifty and had never had children so he was like her baby and she loved spoiling him.

Because he was so anxious about other dogs, Lisa found out about a private field that she could hire at weekends. It was all fenced off so she could take Sherlock off his lead and he could have a run.

The first time she took him, he loved it. There were no other dogs there so he could tear around without worrying. They played ball and he had a mooch around.

Lisa could see how happy he was as his tongue was hanging out and the corners of his mouth had turned up so he looked as if he was smiling. She takes him there every weekend now and it's their happy place.

Over a year on, Lisa is so grateful that she's got Sherlock. They've both been through so much in their lives and they've helped each other to heal. Sherlock is less timid now and he's got his faith back in other people. They're a family and with Sherlock by her side, Lisa knows that she can get through anything.

CHAPTER NINE

Rocco

Gaynor Job watched in amazement as her eighteen-month-old son Dougie climbed into the wooden baby walker.

He sat in the tray part where the bricks usually were and started to propel himself forwards using his hands to turn the wheels.

He looked up at Gaynor and grinned and she could see the determination and delight on his face as he slowly started to move across the floor.

'Clever boy!' she told him.

While most of Dougie's friends had started to toddle about, he was unable to walk so he'd come up with his own ingenious method to get himself around.

When they'd had their twenty-week scan, Gaynor and her

husband Chris had been told that Dougie had club feet. It meant that he would have to have his legs in a cast for a while. Initially the doctors had said he might have some problems walking but that eventually he would be OK.

It had been a shock for them at first but at least they knew what they were dealing with and it was correctable.

But when Dougie had been born, they could see straight away that there was something seriously wrong with his legs and it was much more of an issue than club feet.

His left leg was squashed right up by his face and his right leg was bunched up a bit like a frog's leg.

'Your son has got arthrogryposis,' the consultant had told them a few days later.

It meant that his legs had developed with contractions in the joints and this would affect their ability to move.

Over the first few months of his life, Dougie had faced multiple operations and procedures. Soon after he was born, his legs were put in casts to try and get them into a better position. They'd had to go to Great Ormond Street weekly to get the casts redone.

After that he had an operation to release the tendons in his ankles, which was followed by months of wearing heavy sandals with a bar joining the two shoes together to hold his legs in the same position. He had to wear them twenty-three hours a day for months, including at night, but even so, he still managed to learn to drag himself across the floor with them on. He also had a major operation to move his left leg down from by his face, which meant he had to spend six weeks in a cast from his chest down to his toes.

All of these things were painful and uncomfortable but Gaynor and Chris had been amazed by Dougie's resilience. He was a happy, smiley baby who took everything in his stride and rarely cried or grumbled.

One day they had gone to see the consultant to discuss Dougie's treatment.

'He's never going to be able to walk unaided,' he had told them.

It meant that Dougie was always going to need a wheelchair or a walking frame or crutches to get around.

He'd said it so matter of factly, as if it was more of a passing comment than the life-changing bombshell that it had felt to Gaynor and Chris at the time.

It was devastating but now, watching her son wheel himself round the room in the wooden trolley, Gaynor knew how resilient and determined he was.

As Dougie got older, his attitude didn't change. He just got on with things and Gaynor and Chris knew their role was to try and help him live as full a life as he could and to help him do all the things he wanted to do.

His older sister Tessa was two when Dougie was born. They'd never really sat down and spoken to her about Dougie's legs and what it meant. To her, Dougie was just

Dougie and she accepted him for who he was. The two of them were best friends and they'd often find her stroking his hair or see her doing little things to help him without even realizing it.

When Dougie turned two, he had another operation to put a metal plate in his knee. Shortly afterwards they got him a little molded plastic seat with wheels called a ZipZac so he could get used to using his upper body strength to propel himself around, which he absolutely loved.

At three, he was finally big enough for his first wheelchair. He could use it immediately and they didn't have to teach him. A few days after he got it, they had a day trip to the zoo.

As they walked between the different sections, Dougie wheeled ahead of them in his new chair.

'Look at me Mummy!' he yelled as he whizzed down a hill and turned a sharp corner.

He had absolutely no fear. Gaynor was terrified, but she held herself back from stopping him. She and Chris had always vowed to let Dougie find his own way in life and not wrap him up in cotton wool because of his condition. She could see from the big smile on his face how much he was relishing the independence and enjoying the fact that he could suddenly get around quickly.

As he got older, Dougie started to become more aware of his differences. He'd asked Gaynor and Chris questions in the past and they'd always answered him honestly and openly.

He knew that there was something wrong with his legs, that the condition he had was rare and that there wasn't a reason why it had happened.

As he approached school age, he asked Gaynor and Chris the one question that they'd always been expecting.

'Will I ever be able to walk?'

They could see that Dougie was trying to get his head around what the future held for him.

'The doctors have said you can walk with crutches or a walking frame but not ever without them,' Gaynor said.

Dougie didn't really say much at that and appeared to just accept it.

They gradually adapted the house to make it more open plan for Dougie so he could move around more easily. They had a ramp fitted at the front, installed stairlifts as they had a townhouse on several floors and put AstroTurf in the back garden, which was easier for him to move around on than grass. Dougie used his wheelchair when they were out, but at home, he generally pulled himself around on the floor or sometimes he used a walking frame.

Dougie never failed to amaze them with his fierce independence. He would ask for help if he needed it, but he worked out ways to get himself on and off furniture and in and out of the bath.

But there was occasional frustration too. Dougie was nine now and Tessa eleven, and sometimes Gaynor could see that he got annoyed because he couldn't do some of the things that his sister did.

They were walking up the road one day playing hide and seek. Tessa was crouching behind bushes and jumping out at him.

But when it was Dougie's turn, Gaynor could see that he was struggling and getting upset.

'What is it?' she asked him.

'Every bush I hide behind, you can still see my wheelchair,' he told her. 'If I didn't have this I'd be able to hide properly.'

'I know it must be frustrating Dougie,' she told him.

She wanted to acknowledge how he was feeling and not dismiss it.

She knew that at school he got frustrated sometimes too as his peers wanted to run around and play football. However, he had a loyal group of friends who he would hang around with and who would always involve him. They would pull him along with their jackets to make him go faster, or Dougie would let them push him in his chair.

One comment came out of the blue one day without any warning when they were getting in the car to go to school.

'I wish I could walk,' Dougie sighed. 'I *am* happy but I think my life would be better if I could walk.'

It was a hard thing for Gaynor to hear. It broke her heart because she knew there was no answer or anything they could do. Sometimes all she could do was acknowledge that it was rubbish and unfair and give Dougie a hug.

Gaynor prepared herself for a significant talk, but before she could say anything, Dougie had already changed the subject and moved on.

Instead, to help boost his confidence, they got Dougie to focus on the things that he could do and that weren't dependent on him being able to walk. He loved playing wheelchair basketball and he was a talented swimmer. In the water, he felt like he was no different to anyone else; in fact, he was a better swimmer than many able-bodied people. He loved drumming too and also gaming with his friends, which were both activities where his disability didn't matter.

Luckily Gaynor and Chris had a similar mindset and outlook. They both wanted Dougie to do as much as he could, focus on what he could do not what he couldn't, and if there was something he was desperate to try, to find ways to adapt the activity to make it possible.

There was something else that Chris and Gaynor had been talking about for a while to help boost Dougie's confidence – getting a dog.

Gaynor had grown up with dogs and had wanted one for years, although Chris was more of a cat person. But as the children got older, they were keen for both Dougie and Tessa to experience the unconditional love and responsibility that came from having a pet.

'Perhaps we really should get a dog,' Chris said out of the blue one day. 'It would be something for the kids.'

Gaynor went online straight away before he could change his mind. They wanted a rescue dog and the first place that popped into Gaynor's head was Woodgreen as she used to drive past it years ago on her way to work.

She knew they could give a dog a good home and a lot of love so she filled out a form. When *The Dog House* got in touch, Gaynor thought it would be a memorable thing to do and it would help them find the right dog for their family..

When they told Tessa and Dougie about getting a dog they were really excited, so in August 2020, the family headed to Woodgreen.

Because of Dougie's wheelchair they didn't want a huge dog or, indeed, a tiny one that might get run over by the wheels. They wanted a young, active dog but not a puppy as they didn't want to have to go through the chewing, the biting and the training.

'I don't want a pom, I don't want a poodle and I don't want a chihuahua,' Dougie announced to pet advisor Lizzie. 'Pugs are too sad and poodles are too puffy.'

He described how he wanted a dog that he could throw a ball to and tie to his wheelchair so it could pull him along.

'I think you need a fleet of huskies,' laughed Lizzie.

Gaynor mentioned that she'd like a scraggy-looking dog with bushy eyebrows and a beard.

Back in the office, Lizzie searched through the dogs that were available to see if any of them would be a good match.

'Dougie really wants a playful character that he's going to be able to throw a ball for,' she told Helen.

'What about Rocco?' Helen immediately suggested.

The three-year-old Jack Russell had been brought into Woodgreen by his owner who he'd lived with his entire life. She'd come to the difficult and devastating decision to give him up after her health had declined and she had to use a cane to get around. Rocco just wanted to play and she was struggling to look after such an excitable, energetic dog. She'd been in tears as she'd reluctantly said goodbye to him. When she'd left, Rocco had scratched and whimpered at the door.

He did something that staff at Woodgreen called owner searching. It was when a dog who had been brought into them was constantly looking for their owner and it was always heartbreaking to see.

Lizzie had assumed a dog like Rocco would quickly and easily find a new home, but he'd already been rejected twice. Charnelle had first turned down Rocco. Her seven-year-old son, Reay, had loved his playful nature but she was looking for an affectionate dog and unfortunately in the meeting pen, he hadn't shown any interest in her.

When they'd introduced Rocco to Zach who was looking for a dog unfazed by his Tourette's, it had seemed like a perfect match. But his previous dog who had died was a Jack Russell too and Rocco was too much of a sad reminder.

'Rocco is my nightmare dog,' sighed Lizzie. 'He's the nicest little dog that, for some reason, keeps getting passed over.'

He was what was known as a 'sticky dog' – a fantastic dog that for some unknown reason was struggling to find a home.

Rocco was a really active little pup and he wasn't suited to being in kennels long term. He would often jump up at the bars, desperate to get out.

Lizzie could also see that Rocco was starting to give up hope after he'd been rejected so many times. He was such an exuberant, happy, fun-loving dog but also very affectionate and she knew he would make someone the perfect pet.

So when she suggested him to Gaynor and Chris, she was desperately hoping it was going to be third time lucky.

'We've found a little dog that we hope you will all like,' she said.

She told them about Rocco and how much he loved kids.

'The reason we chose him for you is because he's such an outgoing, sociable chap. He likes toys so much that I imagine he's going to go to Dougie straight away and want to play fetch.'

Dougie clapped his hands with excitement and they were all desperate to meet him.

When an eager Rocco came running into the meeting pen wagging his tail, they all smiled. He ran around for a while and then he went over to Tessa. She threw a toy to him and he bolted after it excitedly. When she held a rope in her hands, he ran around with her chasing it and tugging on the other end.

Dougie was watching carefully from the sidelines.

'Mummy I want Rocco to come to me,' he said.

'He will do,' she told him confidently.

They encouraged Dougie to sit down on the floor and they all smiled as Rocco eventually trotted over to him. Dougie offered him a treat and he obediently sat and took it and Dougie squealed with excitement as he threw a toy for him.

'He's the fastest dog ever,' he laughed as Rocco brought it back to him with record speed.

Gaynor sat there watching the children playing with Rocco. She hadn't instantly fallen for him, but even though it wasn't love at first sight, she did think he was very cute. Chris seemed to really like him and she could already see how much the kids loved him.

She'd never thought about a Jack Russell before, but she could tell that he would be perfect for their family. He ticked all their boxes – he was the right size, very active and affectionate.

Dougie had already made his mind up.

'We're having him!' he yelled.

They told Lizzie they were eager to bring him home straight away.

'You've only just met him so go home and have a chat and a think about it,' she advised them.

She desperately wanted Rocco to find a home, but she wanted to make sure it was the right one.

It was only after they'd agreed to take Rocco that they'd learnt his full story.

'He's such a lovely dog,' sighed Gaynor. 'I'm not surprised his owner was devastated to have to give him up.'

She could tell that he'd been loved, well-trained and cared for and after hearing that he'd been rejected twice, it made her even more determined to give him a loving home.

Rocco was all they talked about in the car on the way back to Essex and they all agreed that they wanted him. First thing the next morning, Gaynor called Woodgreen.

'Our feelings haven't changed,' she told Lizzie. 'We definitely want Rocco and please could we come and pick him up today?'

Rocco was in perfect health and he hadn't been mistreated so she agreed there was no reason why he couldn't be rehomed straight away.

'Give us today to sort out the paperwork,' Lizzie asked and so they agreed to collect him the following day.

To Gaynor, Chris, Dougie and Tessa, it felt like the longest day ever. They went shopping for some beds for Rocco to put around the house and some food and toys that they thought he would like.

The following day, Chris drove to Woodgreen to collect him while Gaynor tried to distract the kids by taking then to the park.

They were all sat excitedly in the living room when Chris pulled up with Rocco. They were so happy to see his little face and his jaunty tail.

They brought him in and let him explore.

'Just wait and let him come to you,' Chris told Dougie and Tessa, and eventually he trotted over to all of them for a stroke, wagging his tail.

Dougie and Tessa couldn't wait to take him out into the garden and show Rocco the new toys they'd bought him.

After a couple of minutes, Gaynor heard them screeching with laughter.

'Come and look at this Mummy,' shouted Dougie. 'Rocco's making a funny face.'

She and Chris went outside to see Rocco sat in the middle of the garden, snapping his teeth furiously like a crocodile.

'I think that means he's excited and wants to play,' Chris told them.

From then on, it became known as Rocco's play face. They loved that he was such fun and so comical.

A few minutes later Rocco was making them howl with laughter again as he commando-crawled his way across the Astro-Turf on his belly.

'It must feel nice on his tummy,' laughed Gaynor.

Then he ran round in circles trying to chase his own tail.

This little dog was so full of character and seeing the looks on Dougie and Tess's faces as they howled with laughter, Gaynor knew they had done the right thing.

It was so nice to see them both playing with him and having fun.

It was as if he understood exactly what they were saying.

'Rocco go get your ball,' Dougie told him and off he trotted to get his ball.

He had boundless energy so he only stopped playing when they'd had enough. He was playful but he was really gentle with them too.

'This is exactly what I'd wanted,' Gaynor told Chris as they watched them through the doors into the garden.

It was great for Dougie because with Rocco, it didn't matter that he couldn't walk or that he was in wheelchair. The little dog didn't see him any differently to how he saw Tessa.

They had been worried how Rocco would settle, but right from the first night, he was fine. Gaynor and Chris put a dog bed on the floor in their room and he slept brilliantly.

After a couple of nights, Tessa was desperate to have Rocco in her room.

'Please can Rocco sleep with me tonight?' she asked.

Wherever his bed was, Rocco seemed to settle as long as he was close to someone.

They took him for walks and Dougie worked out, much

to his delight, that if he held the lead, Rocco could pull him in his wheelchair. Even though he was only a little dog, he was extremely strong.

One day they were out when Rocco spotted a cat. As he sprinted off towards it, Dougie followed at high speed, whooping with delight as Rocco pulled him across the grass. Gaynor quickly realized that they were very well-matched – they were both full of energy and fun.

Dougie loved the fact that Rocco accepted him as he was.

Gaynor and Chris bought a holder for the ball so Dougie was able to give it a good throw. Rocco always brought the ball back to him and they taught him how to drop it on the floor right next to Dougie's wheelchair so that he could reach it.

One of the first days he was with them, Rocco got too close to Dougie when the wheelchair was moving and the chair caught the corner of one of his paws. Rocco let out a little whimper and leapt away.

'Is he OK?' asked Dougie, concerned.

'He's absolutely fine,' Chris reassured him.

After that, Rocco became very wheelchair-savvy and he was always very careful when Dougie was moving around in it.

As the days passed, Rocco's affection for them grew and so did Gaynor's bond with him. She'd always wanted a dog but she'd thought they were getting Rocco primarily for the children, so the strength of her bond with him was a lovely unexpected surprise.

When she got home from work, Rocco started to jump into her arms. When he slept with her and Chris, he would leave his bed on the floor and curl up by their feet instead.

One night, Gaynor picked him up, turned him on his back and laid him on her lap like a baby.

'Hello gorgeous,' she smiled.

As she tickled his tummy, she could see Rocco's eyes getting heavier and heavier and eventually he nodded off upside down on her knee. He was such a sweet little dog and in that moment she suddenly realized that she had fallen madly in love with him.

From then on, Rocco was a real mummy's boy and Gaynor absolutely adored him. She loved the walks and the cuddles and just having him around the house. It always made her smile hearing the patter of his little claws on their laminate floor, and when she was working at home, he came and lay by her feet.

While Dougie loved to play with Rocco, Tessa was more tactile with him. Every night she and Gaynor would battle it out over who was going to have Rocco sleep in their room. When he wasn't by Gaynor and Chris's feet, he was curled up on Tessa's bed.

In September, when they'd had Rocco a few weeks, it was time for Tessa and Dougie to go back to school. Dougie loved school, but because of lockdown, he hadn't been there for months and Gaynor could tell that he was feeling nervous going back.

'It will be fine,' she tried to reassure him. 'You'll get to see all of your friends and your teacher.

That night, when she looked in on Dougie before she went to bed, she was surprised to see Rocco curled up on the end of his bed.

'Look,' she whispered to Chris.

Rocco had never slept in Dougie's room before now but it was as if somehow he could sense Dougie's nerves and knew he needed extra reassurance.

When Dougie woke up in the morning, Gaynor could see how proud he was that Rocco had chosen to sleep with him even though he hadn't asked him to.

In a matter of months, Rocco had become part of their family. Wherever they went, Rocco came too. If Gaynor went for a run, Rocco came with her. When they went out on their kayak on the local river, Rocco sat on the front of it.

Dougie had a hand-bike so he and Chris would often go out for a cycle.

'Please can Rocco come with us?' Dougie asked, so Chris got a bungee lead for him and tied it around his waist.

Dougie loved cycling and seeing Rocco running alongside him.

Rocco also enjoyed going camping with them and seemed to find it really relaxing. He enjoyed being outdoors in the fresh air and sitting on people's laps in their camping chairs and nodding off.

They've had Rocco for over a year now and Gaynor couldn't have wished for a more perfect match. He's given both Tessa and Dougie the chance to experience that unconditional love that you feel for a pet. They all have such a strong bond with Rocco, especially Dougie. He can't wait to get in from school every day to see him and he loves showing him off to his friends. Rocco and Dougie get on brilliantly as they're so similar – they're both big personalities and full of energy and fun. Rocco is perfect for them and he's so playful and affectionate. He's the last bit of the puzzle and has completed their family.

Helen Prestage, Pet Advisor

Helen Prestage held the treat out for her dog.

'Come on Bella,' she gently urged her. 'Come and get it.'

The collie-Lab cross was unlike any dog that Helen had ever known and she was devoted to her. She loved trying to train her, walk her and help her to come out of her shell.

It was hard to believe that growing up, Helen had been terrified of dogs. A friend's Labrador had jumped up at her when she was nine and it had left her really fearful. Her brother Matt had always wanted a dog and after begging their parents Pam and David for years, when Helen was nineteen, they'd finally relented.

They'd gone to Woodgreen after Christmas and chosen a six-month-old collie-Lab cross called Bella. She was quite a lot to take on for naïve first-time dog owners. She chased cars, barked at other dogs and was terrified of people. They quickly discovered that she could scale 6-foot fences so Helen's parents had to get all of the fencing in their garden replaced with taller panels.

For Helen, Bella had cured her fear of dogs and she had fallen in love with her. She was so different to the dog that had jumped up at her when she was younger. Bella was so timid and nervous and it made Helen realize that dogs could be just as scared as people.

She took Bella to training classes and it made her want to understand more about why dogs behaved the way they do.

Even though she was away at university now, Helen loved coming back to spend time with her.

After finishing her degree in English Literature, Helen got an office job at a publishing company but her experience of having Bella had inspired her to want to work with dogs. When she saw a job advertised in the kennels at Woodgreen – where Bella had come from – she applied for it and got it.

She was still living at home with her parents so it wasn't practical to get another dog but it was so tempting being surrounded by them all day.

'I really want to foster dogs,' she told her mum Pam.

'That's fine,' Pam told her. 'As long as they get on with Bella.'

For the first three years, Helen had a foster dog pretty much all the time.

When Helen moved in with her boyfriend Alex she couldn't wait to get a dog of their own. It felt like something was missing in her life.

Again, she decided to foster first to see how a dog would fit into their lives. She was at work one day when a new dog that had come in caught her eye.

Jessie was a four-year-old collie cross who'd been brought into Woodgreen as a stray.

'She's so withdrawn,' one of her colleagues told her. 'She seems so sad and sorry for herself.'

While other dogs would jump up at the bars of their kennels demanding attention, Jessie just sat quietly in her bed.

'I think I'll take her home and foster her,' said Helen. 'She doesn't look like she's enjoying living in kennels.'

She knew it would help with Jessie's home assessment that they had to write for prospective adoptees.

As soon as she got Jessie home, she was like a different dog. That first night she curled up happily next to Helen on the sofa. She looked so contented and relaxed and it was then that Helen knew she couldn't take her back.

'I want to keep her,' she told Alex and luckily he felt the same way.

Before Jessie had come along, Helen had been very house-proud and was constantly cleaning and polishing. Jessie shed hair everywhere and she was a messy eater, but Helen didn't care. Having her own dog at last immediately made their house feel like a home.

Helen had instantly fallen in love with Jessie. She reminded her so much of Bella – she loved her intelligence and how human her eyes were. When Jessie looked at her, Helen felt like she was looking into her soul.

Helen soon discovered that Jessie's main love in life was running off lead and it wasn't easy getting her to come back. She took her to training classes to try and teach her recall and even did some one-to-one sessions with her colleague Sue to see if that would help.

But she knew it would make Jessie miserable to stop her, so they were just very careful about where they allowed her to do it.

One afternoon Helen took her for a walk to one of their favourite places. It was a huge field behind a hospital and it was all fenced off so it was popular with dog walkers.

As soon as Helen let her off her lead, Jessie shot off. She loved sniffing her way around the whole place. Helen could normally see her in the distance and she always came back.

But on this particular day, she didn't.

'Jessie!' shouted Helen, pacing up and down. 'Jessie where are you?'

She searched for her for ages but couldn't see any sign of her.

As time went on, Helen started to get a funny feeling. All

her instincts were telling her that something terrible had happened.

She knew that on the other side of the fence there was a bank that led down to a busy dual carriageway.

Helen's heart started to race as she ran over to that side of the field. As she ran up and down through the bushes, she saw it – a small hole in the fence. She climbed through it and fought her way through the undergrowth and down the embankment towards the busy road.

'Jessie,' she pleaded, as cars shot past. 'Where are you? Please come back.'

But it was too late.

Much to her horror, Helen saw a shape lying by the side of the road that she knew instinctively was Jessie.

She'd made it over one part of the dual carriageway but had been hit by a car on the other side. Someone must have stopped and kindly moved her body off the road.

Helen was desperate to get to her and hold her in her arms but it was too dangerous to try and cross.

They'd only had her for eight months and Helen was devastated.

'It's all my fault,' she sobbed to Alex that night.

'There was nothing you could have done,' he reassured her.

She cried as she cleared away Jessie's bed and her favourite toys.

Helen had never lost anyone that close to her before and

the shock and the devastation were horrendous. She felt so guilty too. It had been her job to protect Jessie and keep her safe and she felt like she'd let her down.

As part of her job at Woodgreen, Helen got three days pet bereavement leave. She went back after two because she wanted to be in the kennels with the dogs. Work was a great distraction and being able to cuddle and care for other dogs made her feel like Jessie was still with her somehow.

Helen hated coming home from work and opening the door to complete silence. She had loved being the centre of Jessie's world and having someone who relied on her for everything.

Helen spoke to Alex about looking for a new dog straight away.

'I think we should get two,' she told him. 'I can't bear the pain of losing a dog again and not having another dog there.'

Thankfully he felt the same.

Over the next few months, they fostered several dogs but none of them were quite right.

Perhaps they just weren't ready and were trying to force it, Helen thought. She was convinced that when she met the right dogs she would know, and it would heal their broken hearts and help them to move on from what happened with Jessie.

When a collie cross came in to be rehomed, Helen jumped at the chance to foster her. Susie had been living as a stray and then she had been rehomed, but her owner had left her outside for nine hours a day. She hated being cold and had barked constantly so had been brought into Woodgreen. But despite everything that she'd been through, she was so happy and sociable.

They'd only been fostering her for a few days when a nine-month-old mongrel called Amber came into Woodgreen. She was a skinny stray who had been hit by a car and Helen's heart melted when she first saw this tiny, terrified thing.

Staff had managed to get her into a kennel when she first arrived but now they couldn't get her out. Helen spent hours sat at the front of the kennel trying to tempt her out but she'd gone into complete shutdown and nothing worked.

Amber had pressed herself into the far corner of the kennel and she kept ducking away when Helen tried to slip a lead over her head. She didn't want to have to crawl in and physically wrench her out because she knew that would make her even more traumatized.

Then she had an idea.

'I'm going to see if Susie can help,' she told a colleague.

Because she was fostering Susie she was able to bring her to work with her. Helen went and got Susie and they sat outside Amber's kennel.

Within a few minutes, Amber got up and came out to see Susie. As she sniffed her up and down, her was tail wagging.

'I think I'm going to ask to foster Amber too,' Helen told her colleague.

They'd only had Susie a few days but judging by their first meeting, Helen could tell that she could really help to bring Amber out of her shell and get her ready for rehoming.

The pair of them clicked straight away. Amber wasn't house-trained, she didn't know how to walk on a lead and was terrified of everything. Susie taught her how to be a dog so Helen didn't have to.

Amber didn't understand how to play or have fun but when she saw Helen throwing the ball to Susie and her running after it, she wanted to do it too.

They were the perfect mix of personalities and after a few weeks, Helen knew she couldn't split them up. So they rehomed both of them.

Helen knew they'd never forget Jessie but with Amber and Susie to lavish their love on, they could finally start to move on.

Helen couldn't wait to push open the front door and be greeted by two wagging tails and lots of kisses. No matter how hard her day had been, they always made it better . She still got upset about Jessie and if she was ever tearful, Susie would come over and put her head on her lap and it would bring her instant comfort.

Three years after they'd got the dogs, Helen and Alex got married and a couple of years later their daughter Isabella was born.

Helen knew having a new baby in the house was going to be a big change for the dogs. She got advice from her colleagues at Woodgreen and did her best to prepare them. Her brother Matt had recently had a baby so they had experience of being around young children and had been fine. On the night Isabella was born, Alex took a blanket home from the hospital and put it near Amber and Susie's beds so that they could get used to her smell.

Helen was particularly worried about Amber as she was so sensitive but they made sure they kept their routine exactly the same and fed and walked them at the same time. Thankfully, after Isabella was born things seemed to be fine. Neither of the dogs seemed particularly interested in Isabella and her crying didn't bother them. Helen had been worried so it was such a relief.

The problems came as Isabella got older and started moving around. Helen could tell both dogs were unsure of this creature suddenly crawling around on the floor towards them.

Amber would take herself off to another part of the house for some peace and quiet but Susie always liked to be by Helen's side.

Helen made sure she always watched them when they were together. Isabella was eight months old when she was crawling around the kitchen floor one afternoon. Susie was lying there, having a rest, with one eye open watching what was going on.

Before Helen could stop her, Isabella had crawled right over to Susie's bed and had reached out and grabbed her. Suddenly Susie raised her head, let out a growl and snapped at Isabella.

Isabella burst into tears and Helen quickly ran over and scooped her up.

'Oh you poor thing,' she said, trying to comfort her.

Much to Helen's horror, Susie's teeth had caught Isabella's eye and she had three scratches. A few minutes later, her whole eye was red and swollen.

Isabella was hysterical and Susie, sensing that she'd done something to upset Helen, slunk off with her tail between her legs.

Helen was in shock. She was devastated and blamed herself for not getting in there quick enough. That night she talked about it with Alex.

'Are we putting Isabella in danger?' she sighed. 'What if Susie hurts her again?'

Next time it could be much more serious. Helen felt caught in the middle. Isabella was too young to understand that dogs needed space but she also knew that it was hard for Susie. She'd had her and Alex for most of her life and now there was this little being wriggling around, making loads of noise and pulling at her. It was no wonder that she'd snapped.

Helen felt so guilty.

'Are we doing the right thing by her?' she worried to Alex.

'They'll get used to each other eventually,' he reassured her.

Helen desperately hoped that he was right.

In the meantime, she couldn't take any chances so she put up a baby gate to separate Susie from Isabella.

When Isabella was awake, Susie had to be on the other side of the baby gate.

When she napped, that was Helen's time with Susie when she would play with her and cuddle her.

Helen was desperate for them all to get on. She wanted that dream of the kids, the dogs, everyone going out for walks together and cuddling up on the sofa.

To have to physically remove Susie and put a barrier between them was really hard. Helen felt guilty that she was putting Susie through this but also she didn't want her daughter to put the dog in a situation where she felt like she had to snap.

Helen didn't want Susie to feel like she was taking her away and punishing her so she gave her treats and toys to play with.

Helen had seen this situation so many times at Woodgreen and she knew that many dogs were given up because they'd reacted negatively to a new baby. She was secretly worried that eventually she would have to do the same. The thought of giving up Susie after all those years was unthinkable but Helen knew they also had to consider her daughter's safety.

All they could do was hope that things would get easier. They'd had Susie for five years before they'd had children so Helen felt like they owed it to her to try everything possible.

But as the months passed, nothing seemed to change. Isabella was a typical toddler, wanting to grab and pull everything so Helen continued to keep her and the dogs separate.

By the time Isabella was walking, Helen took her out into the garden with Susie to try and teach her how to stroke her.

'Gentle,' she said as she showed Isabella how to stroke Susie.

But before she could stop her, Isabella suddenly grabbed Susie's tail and pulled it. She held on so tightly, Helen couldn't wrench her hand off and Susie swung her head around and snapped at her. She caught Isabella on her face again but thankfully this time there was only a small red mark.

Helen felt like they were back to square one again but her colleagues reassured her.

'Remember it's not going to be forever,' one of her colleagues told her and Helen clung onto that.

They had to keep persevering.

Yes, Susie had snapped at Isabella again but Helen could totally see why.

There was still that nagging worry at the back of her mind though about what if it did happen again and next time it was more serious? All Helen could do was keep Isabella separate from the dogs and watch them like a hawk if they were ever together.

As Isabella got older and learnt to talk, she started to be able to understand more.

'Be gentle with Susie,' Helen told her.

She tried to explain to her that Susie didn't like being grabbed or climbed on as that hurt her and made her cross. Instead, Helen tried to show her what Susie did like.

She encouraged Isabella to help care for Susie so she was the one who put her food out in the bowl or fed her a treat. When they went on a walk, they would let Isabella help them hold her lead.

Helen did everything she could to try and build up positive associations between her and Susie.

They took her out into the garden one day.

'Susie loves her ball,' Helen smiled. 'I bet she'd really like it if you threw it for her.'

Isabella threw it and Susie bounded after it which made Isabella laugh. She loved it when Susie dropped it back by her feet.

It was all very gradual but slowly Helen could see things starting to change. Isabella had started to understand that Susie didn't like her doing certain things and, in turn, Susie had started to get used to Isabella.

If Isabella made a loud a noise or she'd throw a toy, Susie would open one eye and instead of being startled she'd realize what it was and go back to sleep.

As Isabella got older, Helen taught her what the dogs did or didn't like. Isabella then liked to tell everyone, including Helen and Alex, how to behave around Susie.

'Don't touch Susie when she's in her bed or lying down on the sofa,' she told them. 'She doesn't like it.'

'And don't touch Amber when she's eating because she might get a bit grumpy.'

When their son Isaac was born, three years later, Susie was like a different dog. She'd found her confidence and she'd learnt to trust the children and she knew they weren't going to hurt her.

It was such a huge relief for Helen. Now Susie is Isabella's favourite and they have a mutual respect for each other and such a strong bond.

When they get home after school, Isabella, who is now five, will run to Susie first. The other day Helen went into the living room to find them curled up on the sofa together watching a movie.

Helen has been at Woodgreen for fourteen years and she knows she couldn't have got through the past few years without the support of her colleagues. It also gave her a greater understanding of the many families that find themselves in a similar situation and are not so lucky to have people who can advise them on what to do. She knows if she hadn't worked at Woodgreen and rehomed dogs with similar issues, then she would have probably been convinced to rehome Susie. There were times Helen thought Susie was going to be terrified of children forever and they'd ruined her life. There were times when she feared it wasn't going to get any better and they might have to do the unthinkable and give Susie up. But with love, perseverance and help from her colleagues, they finally got through it and she's so grateful.

CHAPTER TEN

Joey

Head down, Holly Pullen walked up the aisles of the super-market towards the till for the start of her shift, praying that no one would speak to her.

Too late.

Her heart sank as a woman approached her.

'Excuse me,' she said. 'Can you tell me where the cat food is?'

Holly felt herself getting hot and her heart was racing so fast, it felt like it was going to burst out of her chest. She stared down at the floor, willing this person to just go away. Panic filled her body and she wanted to run.

Even though she worked at the supermarket and knew the answer, Holly couldn't find the words. She feared that if she spoke, gibberish would come out of her mouth.

'I-I – er . . .' she stammered, unable to get the words out.

She promptly burst into tears. As Holly scurried off down the aisle, the woman looked after her as if she were mad.

That was the moment that Holly knew she had to face facts. Her mental health had got so bad that it had come to a tipping point. She realized she could no longer hold down a job and work in this supermarket. She handed in her notice and went home in floods of tears.

Holly had always felt different. Growing up, she'd struggled to make friends and was always a bit of a loner.

When she'd hit her teenage years, her emotions had been all over the place. Everyone had put her extreme mood swings down to hormones and said she was being a drama queen.

One minute she would be laughing hysterically, the next the sadness was so overwhelming, Holly felt as if her world had ended.

'What's wrong?' her mum would ask her, worried, as she cried and refused to get out of bed.

But that was the hard part. Holly didn't know why she felt that way.

When she'd left school, Holly had worked as a singer at a holiday camp. Even though she struggled to interact with people, on stage performing she felt like a different person. It was as if she was playing a part, like it wasn't really her and her onstage persona was an escape from the stress she felt in her everyday life.

In 2013 she'd met Adam. He'd been on holiday with his family and he had come over to chat to her after the show and compliment her on what a good voice she had. They'd kept in touch on Facebook and a week later, he'd asked her out and driven all the way from Essex to take her on a date. They'd been together for a week and a half when Holly had told him that she loved him and a year later they were married. Their son Oscar was born in 2014.

Holly had eventually been diagnosed with anxiety and depression and given medication but nothing seemed to help with her extreme mood swings. Now, barely even able to have a conversation in the supermarket with a stranger, Holly knew there was something else wrong with her.

Even after she'd given up work, things continued to get worse. Any social situation filled her with anxiety and she was constantly worried about what she would do or say.

When Oscar had just started nursery, Holly took him to one of his new friend's birthday parties. As he happily ran around the church hall, Holly sat there alone, feeling terrified and hoping no one would try and speak to her.

'Hello, how are you?' said one of the mums coming to sit down next to her. 'You're Oscar's mum, aren't you?'

Holly knew she was only being friendly but she felt panic rising in her chest and she burst into tears.

'Oh my goodness. I'm so sorry, are you OK?' the woman asked, clearly concerned. 'What's wrong?'

That made it even worse. How could Holly tell her that she didn't actually know what was wrong with her or why she was crying?

The mood swings coupled with her anxiety and depression got worse and in 2017, Holly hit rock bottom. She felt overwhelmed and didn't want to be here any more. A family bereavement followed by panic attacks so severe that they made her pass out, pushed Holly over the edge and led her to try and take her own life.

In Holly's head, that night was all a blur.

Adam calling the ambulance . . . a kind paramedic giving her a hug and reassuring her that it would all be OK . . . the flashing blue light of the ambulance as she was rushed to hospital.

The next thing she knew, Holly woke up in a bed on a mental health ward. For the first time in a long time, she felt relieved. Over the next two weeks, she talked to countless medical staff about how she'd been feeling.

'I'm sure there's something else wrong with me that can't just be explained by anxiety and depression,' Holly told the doctor. 'My moods and emotions are so up and down all the time.'

Eventually they had an answer.

'You've got something called emotionally unstable personality disorder, or EUPD,' the consultant explained.

He described her mind as being a bit like a tombola. When

people experience a happy situation or a sad situation, their brain gives them the right emotions. Whereas Holly's brain was like a tombola and it would just give her a random emotion at a random time. It meant that she would never know how she was going to be or react at any given time. So she might laugh at a funeral or cry at a happy occasion like a party or a birthday without having any control over it. Her emotions could vary and switch very quickly several times a day.

For Holly, it was a huge relief to have a diagnosis. Suddenly everything made sense and she had a reason for why she reacted so bizarrely in certain situations. She wasn't strange, crazy or weird, she had an illness. Her problems were still there but she understood it a bit more, rather than constantly berating herself and worrying about what was wrong with her.

Unfortunately, like most mental health conditions, EUPD isn't curable. Medication and therapy could help the anxiety and depression side of it but Holly knew there wasn't a pill that she could take to help her moods or the way she was feeling.

Her moods could change up to twenty times a day and it was exhausting for Adam as he never knew which Holly he was going to get. It was hard to cope with the extreme highs and lows and sometimes it felt like he had two children to take care of.

One morning he woke up and Holly was so full of energy, she barely knew what to do with herself.

'Morning,' she beamed. 'I feel great today.'

She was like a child who had eaten a bag of sweets; she was so hyperactive, she was bouncing off the walls.

'Calm down,' Adam told her. 'Come and sit down or you'll burn yourself out.'

'I can't,' she smiled.

Ten minutes later, Adam found Holly curled up in a ball on their bed, sobbing.

'Please go away,' she told him.

It was hard for him to see her so upset and distressed and know that there was nothing that he could do to help.

Holly's anxiety got so bad that she struggled to be left alone in the house. As her moods got more extreme, Adam had to take time off work to look after her. It got to the point where he had to stop working and become Holly's full-time carer, as she was registered disabled.

Holly got so fearful, she started to avoid most social situations. If she was surrounded by a lot of people, she always felt really uncomfortable. She would sit there in silence and was too scared to speak. She was worried that she was going to panic or act in the wrong way or say something inappropriate, and they wouldn't understand that she had no control over it.

Ordinary situations like going to the shops or doing the school run got so difficult that Holly stopped leaving the house. She couldn't have a routine or make plans because she didn't know how she was going to feel when she woke up on a morning.

She loved being a mum but she felt guilty about the impact that her condition had on Oscar. She couldn't drop him off at school or take him on days out or to parties.

Adam did his best to keep things normal for Oscar but the little boy understood that his mum was ill.

When they pulled up outside a shop one afternoon in the car, he told Adam: 'Mummy can't go in there because it stresses her out.'

Holly felt guilty that he was so aware of her issues. He was so helpful, it broke her heart. He knew that Mummy had a poorly brain and she couldn't be around people and he was really understanding when they went places as a family. As Adam went into the shop, Oscar grabbed Holly's hand.

'It's OK Mummy,' he told her. 'Don't worry, I'm here with you.'

In the long days at home when Oscar was at school, Holly took solace in the online world. She found meeting people virtually a lot less stressful than in real life.

She set up Facebook and TikTok accounts in the name of Jolly Holly. She missed her old life being a singer and getting up on stage and performing, so being 'Jolly Holly' was her outlet. She told jokes, made people laugh and helped to raise money to buy toys for disadvantaged children for Christmas.

She also talked about her mental health and her struggles

with EUPD. Holly liked being open about it and people contacted her to say they suffered from EUPD as well, and it helped her to know that she wasn't alone.

But sometimes Holly's mood swings meant she didn't feel like going online and at those times, the days felt long and hard.

For a while, she and Adam had been talking about getting a dog. Holly knew that not only would it be a companion for her, but Oscar would love it too. He was six now and could be quite hyperactive at times. Holly worried that it was because they spent so much time at home because of her condition.

She knew that, as an only child, he was missing a little brother or sister to play with. For the past few years, she and Adam had desperately wanted another baby. Holly had been diagnosed with polycystic ovaries and a hormone imbalance at the age of nineteen and was warned she might find it difficult to get pregnant. She had got pregnant with Oscar straight away but, as the years had passed, she hadn't been able to conceive again. She felt guilty about not being able to give him a sibling and, even though she knew a dog wasn't a replacement for a baby, she thought it would help him feel less lonely.

'Would you like us to get a doggy?' she asked him one day and Oscar's face lit up.

'It can be my best friend Mummy,' he told her.

Holly was on Facebook one day when she came across a post about a TV show that caught her attention.

Are you looking for a dog to help you or your family?

She was particularly interested in the fact that it said a team of specialist people would work with you to find the right dog for your family.

'Do you think it's worth a try?' she asked Adam.

They'd never had a dog before and they didn't know where to start. Understandably, she was nervous about getting it wrong. Holly knew she didn't want a huge dog that could pull her over but she didn't have a particular breed in mind.

'I just want something cuddly, friendly and fluffy that will just sit on my lap and comfort me.'

Holly wanted the dog to be her friend and also be good with Oscar.

They filled out the application form agreeing to take part and in May 2019, they headed to Woodgreen and told pet advisor Helen how they were looking for a dog that could be part of their family.

'I've always wanted a dog and it would be good to have this bundle of bouncy happiness,' Holly told her. 'I'd like one that's happy to be there and will sit on my lap.'

She explained that she had emotional problems and how she thought it would be helpful for her to have an extra little friend.

Holly thought she was excited but Oscar was literally bouncing up and down at the thought of getting a dog.

Holly explained how guilty she felt about not being able to get out of the house much.

'Oscar can be very hyperactive and I feel like it's my fault because we don't really get out of the house a lot. I'm hoping taking the dog for walk will help both him and us.'

The staff knew how much was riding on this dog but were concerned it may be too much for an animal to take on.

'She really wants a dog who's able to read her moods,' said Helen.

One dog immediately sprung to mind – seven-month-old Joey. He was a collie cross who'd been abandoned in the countryside but he was very confident, affectionate and sociable. Helen knew collies were generally very sensitive to people's moods so she was hopeful that he would be a good match for Holly.

When Joey had first come into Woodgreen, he'd been paired up with a nervous collie called Kimmy. Joey had helped to bring her out of her shell and the pair of them used to love to play and cuddle up together at night. Recently Kimmy had been adopted and now staff were keen for Joey to find his own loving home too.

Helen went to tell the family the good news.

'We did find one dog. His name is Joey and he's a little mongrel. He's very cute and because of your situation, he could be a real lifeline in terms of getting out and meeting other dog walkers. He's super social.'

As they waited in the meeting pen, Holly's heart was racing. She knew there was so much depending on how this meeting went. She desperately wanted it to work out, because she could see how excited Oscar was and really didn't want to let him down.

When Joey ran into the pen, Holly immediately fell in love. He was small, fluffy and incredibly cute – in fact everything that she had ever wanted.

'Oh my God this is the best day of my life,' she sighed.

'I'm not sure who's more excited – you or Oscar,' laughed Adam.

As ever, Holly's emotions were a rollercoaster. As she watched Oscar laughing as he chased Joey around the pen, she couldn't stop herself from bursting into tears. The next minute, her cheeks hurt from smiling so much.

'You are so adorable,' she told Joey as she gave him a stroke.

Holly didn't have any doubts at all about adopting Joey. She instantly knew that he was going to bring so much joy to their home and she hoped that, in return, they could shower him with love and give him a happy life too.

'We'll take him,' she told Helen without any hesitation.

Holly and Adam had always said that if they got a rescue dog, they would want to choose its name. So on the drive back from Woodgreen, they discussed some options. They both loved video games so they suggested Sonic or Mario, but neither sounded right. Then Holly thought about her favourite film *Labyrinth*. She was obsessed with it and one of her favourite characters was a monster named Ludo.

'Please can we call him that?' she implored, and thankfully Adam agreed.

Holly's nerves didn't kick in until they brought Ludo home three weeks later. She was worried that he wouldn't like them as much as they liked him.

Woodgreen staff had warned them that he might be timid at first. They put a large metal cage downstairs and put a cosy dog bed in it and a blanket over the top so it was dark. For the first few days, Ludo kept running over and hiding in his sanctuary. However, as each day passed, he spent less and less time in there.

Holly's big wish had been for their dog to be a friend for her. She knew how stressful it could be for Adam looking after her all the time. She didn't ever go out and she didn't have a lot of friends or family for support. She thought having a little buddy in the house would help her, but Holly was also realistic. Ludo had been through enough in his own life and she knew she couldn't rely on him to solve her problems.

However, Ludo turned out to be the most friendly and loving dog Holly had ever met. From the very beginning, he would jump up on the sofa next to her and sit on her lap.

A couple of days after Ludo arrived, Holly felt herself getting very anxious. Sometimes, for no reason, she would start to feel worried and stressed and she had that familiar overwhelming sense of panic rising in her chest.

'What's wrong?' asked Adam. 'What can I do?'

'Nothing,' snapped Holly.

At times like these when she was stressed, she tended to push Adam away.

She went and sat in the living room to try and get control of her breathing. As she sat on the sofa, she noticed Ludo watching her out of the corner of his eye. A few seconds later, he jumped up next to her and sat on her lap.

He gently rested his head on her chest and looked up at her.

Holly stared into his brown eyes and she felt her heart swell with love. It was as if he was trying to help her calm down – and it was working.

'You are just too adorable,' she told him.

She remembered someone telling her that collies were very intuitive and connected to people's emotions, and seeing the way Ludo had come over to her to comfort her, she definitely believed it. One look at his cute face and her heart just melted.

A few minutes later, Holly got up and took Ludo out into the garden where she threw his ball to him.

Ludo was the friendliest dog she had ever known, but that was both a blessing and a curse when they took him out for walk. Holly had hoped that getting a dog would encourage her to leave the house a bit more. She was too anxious to go out with him alone but she wanted them to go on walks as a family or for Adam to accompany them in the daytime when Oscar was at school.

But the first time she and Adam took him out for a walk, Holly was filled with panic.

'What if we meet someone and Ludo wants to go over to them?' she agonized.

'We'll make sure we walk somewhere remote and it will be fine,' Adam reassured her.

Luckily they were surrounded by open countryside so Holly was reassured that they'd find a secluded route.

However, a few minutes after setting off, Holly's stomach started to churn as she saw another couple approaching them with their dog. This was what she'd been dreading.

Holly's breathing started to get shallower and she started to worry that she would get so anxious that she would pass out.

Ludo was straining at the lead, desperate to go and say hello to the other dog heading towards them.

'Please Adam,' she whispered. 'What are we going to do?'

People always said that getting a dog was very social and it was a great way to meet new people but, for Holly, it was her worst nightmare. Ludo was so friendly he wanted to say hello to absolutely everyone, but Holly found it terribly hard to talk to strangers. If she was forced to talk to the older couple walking towards them, Holly was worried that she'd panic and say something odd or inappropriate.

'I'll take him over,' Adam told her.

He led a delighted Ludo over while Holly stood half hidden behind some bushes. She could see the couple looking over at her, slightly puzzled that she wasn't coming over to speak to them too. Ludo was enjoying himself as he excitedly gave their Labrador a sniff and jumped up to say hello to this couple.

Over the past few years, Holly had got to the point where she hardly ever went out unless she was going to see her mum. They did their food shop online and Adam took Oscar to school. Now, for the first time, Ludo had encouraged her to leave the house but Adam was worried it would put Holly off from ever going out with Ludo again.

Over the next few weeks, they searched for the most deserted footpaths and remote walks where they could take Ludo. On the rare occasion they did see someone coming towards them, they would quickly go off in a different direction.

It really helped Holly to have a daily dose of fresh air, exercise and a change of scene. Walking Ludo helped to calm her mind and on good days, they would go out for over an hour.

Ludo was always there for Holly whenever she felt stressed or upset. One afternoon, she was having a particularly bad day. Her moods had been up and down and she was already exhausted. At times like these, she was overwhelmed by an unbearable sadness and she would sit in her room and cry for days.

What's the point in life? she asked herself as she lay on the bed in tears.

'Please leave me alone,' she told Adam when he came to check on her.

On really down days, she tended to push her family away. A few minutes later, Ludo ran into the room. He jumped up onto the bed and snuggled up into Holly's chest. He lay there next to her for ages, perfectly quiet and still.

It brought her so much comfort and it made her feel like someone did care. When no one else was able to cheer her up, Ludo seemed to know exactly what she needed.

Ludo quickly became the constant companion Holly had craved.

Adam rarely left Holly alone but he had to go and collect Oscar from school every day. As soon as he left, Holly felt very anxious as she always struggled being on her own in the house.

One afternoon he'd been gone for ten minutes, when there was a knock at the door. Without Adam there to answer it, it immediately sent Holly spiralling into a panic. Her constant worry was that she was going to have a panic attack and then pass out.

Sensing something was wrong, Ludo immediately jumped into her lap. Holly closed her eyes and stroked his fur, willing the person at the door to go away. Instead of having a full-blown panic attack, she managed to breathe her way through it and stop her heart from racing. She was too scared to move so she sat like that until Adam came home. Every day life was exhausting for her but Ludo always helped.

Holly liked the fact that the feeling was mutual. If Ludo was stressed or upset, he would come to her for comfort. If Oscar was being too boisterous or if Ludo was tired and didn't want to play any more, he would come and curl up behind Holly's legs. He was terrified of the vacuum and whenever Adam got it out of the cupboard, Ludo would immediately leap into Holly's lap and snuggle up.

She was his protector just as much as he was hers.

Ludo was so intuitive, there were also times he knew to stay away from Holly and give her some space. Sometimes she would get frustrated over something silly. Like the morning she tried to make herself and Adam a cup of tea and managed to burn herself on the kettle and drop the cup. Even something as minor as that was enough to send Holly's mood spiraling. It made her feel like a failure and she got angry and upset.

'I'm so stupid,' Holly berated herself. 'I can't even do something simple like make a cup of tea.'

She let out a loud grunt of frustration and Ludo knew to make himself scarce. Frustrated, Holly took herself off for a self-enforced time out. She went into her bedroom for twenty minutes to listen to some music and to try and calm down. As soon as she lay down on the bed, Ludo came trotting back for a cuddle. He was really good at reading what kind of mood she was in and always knew exactly what she needed. Ludo didn't judge her and he loved her for who she was, which meant so much to Holly.

She loved the relationship he had with Oscar too. If Oscar was ever crying, Ludo would jump on his lap and Oscar would cuddle him. He helped him burn off steam by running around in the garden with him and then afterwards they'd sit together and watch TV. Oscar introduced Ludo to people as his 'little brother'.

Ludo is three now and Holly feels he's changed her life completely. Because of Ludo, Holly is the most active she has been in years. She walks him every day and runs round in the garden with him, throwing him a ball. Since they've got him she's lost four stone and is hoping to lose more so she can be put on medication to help her polycystic ovaries and, hopefully, she will be able to have another baby.

For Adam, Ludo has brought him peace of mind. It was always so frustrating for him not knowing how to help Holly when she was struggling but he can see how much comfort Ludo brings her. Whenever she's down, Ludo is by her side and Adam can see she's much more balanced. With Ludo around, their house is a much happier place.

Holly never knows what mood each day is going to bring. All she can do is face it one day at a time. She's learnt to make the most of the good days and live in the moment. Her condition still means life is exhausting, but with Ludo by her side, she has the constant, non-judgmental companion that she's always wanted.

CHAPTER ELEVEN

Bluebell

Sharron Fraser-Smith felt a pang of grief in her chest as she gazed at the empty spot next to her on the sofa. It was a space that had been taken up by her chocolate-brown Labrador, Talia, or Taz for short. For thirteen years, everywhere Sharron had gone, Taz had come too. She was her wingman; they were like Batman and Robin.

Sharron is a trauma nurse in the Royal Navy and Taz would come to work with her at the headquarters in Plymouth where she was appointed as a Training Officer and Deputy Officer Commanding Nursing. She would lie under Sharron's desk and everyone would make a fuss of her or feed her biscuits. She was a great therapy dog if the students were feeling stressed and she became the headquarter's unofficial mascot.

Sharron lived alone and was resolutely single so Taz had been her constant companion and much more reliable than any man had ever been. A brief five-month marriage and, years before that, a man who had turned out to be married, had destroyed both her confidence and her trust in the opposite sex. She didn't need a relationship or a man in her life when she had Taz.

Sadly, Taz had developed hip problems and quickly lost her mobility. Then she was diagnosed with aggressive cancer in her claw that kept returning. Finally, just before her thirteenth birthday in April 2019, Sharron could see that Taz had had enough. Her quality of life had deteriorated so much that Sharron was forced to make the decision that she had always been dreading. Just before midnight, the vet arrived and she held Taz in her arms as she was put to sleep.

For the past few months, Sharron had been lost in a thick fog of grief. Now, even sitting on the sofa watching TV didn't feel right without Taz lying next to her.

She hated the quiet the most, coming home to an empty house and the constant, deafening silence. At times like this, the grief felt overwhelming and Sharron sat on the sofa and sobbed.

'I miss you so much Taz,' she sighed aloud.

Her house no longer felt like a home any more without Taz in it and she took no pleasure in being there. Sharron's whole life had revolved around her beloved dog. Wherever she had gone, Taz had come too and at night she slept in her bed with her. Sometimes, if Sharron closed her eyes, she was convinced that she could still hear her panting and the patter of her paws on the tiled kitchen floor.

Taz was her fur baby, her big chocolate bear, and Sharron had loved her like she was her little girl. Life without her was incredibly lonely.

Over the next few months, Sharron threw herself into her work so she didn't have time to think about anything else.

'Why don't you get another dog?' her parents Wendy and Michael suggested but she refused.

'I can't do it,' she told them firmly. 'I can't go through that again.'

Sharron was absolutely adamant that she wasn't going to get another dog. She couldn't fall in love with another animal and then watch them be in pain and have to make that terrible decision to put them down. Her heart couldn't take it.

She still missed being around dogs so she offered to walk some of her neighbours' dogs. That way she could still get her doggy fix without the emotional attachment.

By October 2019, Sharron was still grieving for Taz but it wasn't as intense and overwhelming any more. Slowly, she was getting used to life without a dog being around.

One night she was going out to meet her sister Amanda. She dashed upstairs in a pair of stilettoes and as she ran, her foot clipped the top step. Sharron felt herself toppling forwards so she tried to readjust herself to avoid falling flat on her face on the landing.

But she overcompensated, lost her balance completely and, much to her horror, fell backwards down the stairs. She heard the thuds and felt the impact as her spine hit the edge of each and every one of the thirteen steps on the way down. She ended up, dazed and confused, lying on her back at the foot of the stairs.

When she eventually came around from the shock, Sharron realized that she could move her legs, but not her back. She was in terrible agony. Alone and scared, she reached for her mobile phone that luckily she still had in the pocket of her trousers. She didn't want to cause a fuss so she called 111. When she heard what was wrong, the woman on the end of the line immediately said: 'I'll call you an ambulance.'

At the hospital, a scan appeared to show that thankfully it was just soft tissue damage. But over the next few days, Sharron was convinced she had sustained a much more serious injury in the fall. She was in so much pain, she couldn't get upstairs so she was forced to sleep on a swivel chair in the living room. She was getting worse rather than better and, nearly two weeks later, she could only crawl around on all fours. She couldn't walk or sit up straight and she was starting to lose sensation down one side of her body. Her nursing training told her that something major was wrong.

Sharron went to see a Navy physiotherapist but he couldn't treat her because she was in too much pain.

'This isn't right,' he told her.

He sent her to see her GP who referred her straight to the spinal unit at the hospital. Sharron had more tests and scans and was examined again. She hobbled out to the waiting room and was getting her jacket on to go home when the consultant came out to see her.

'Where are you going?' he asked.

'I presumed I was going home,' she said but he shook his head.

'We need to admit you right now,' he told her. 'You've broken your spine.'

Sharron was horrified to hear that she had seven fractures in total. One vertebra had five fractures in it. And because she'd been trying to move around because she thought it was only soft tissue damage, her spine had collapsed above the original fracture so she was going to be left with permanent damage.

There were two options – surgery or a body brace. Sharron didn't want to risk an operation or a subsequent infection in her spine so she chose the second.

Her treatment involved wearing a spinal brace for twenty-four hours a day for six months and lots of rest. The metal and plastic brace was like a thick, heavy jacket that Sharron wore over her clothes to keep her spine stable so the fractures could heal.

She was housebound and at first she couldn't walk so she moved in with her parents.

One night she woke up in agony. The pain was horrendous and the brace was hot, uncomfortable and hard to sleep in.

Desperate for some relief, Sharron tried to reach for the liquid morphine on the bedside table but she couldn't get to it.

'Mum,' she cried out. 'Please help me.'

She had always been such a fiercely independent person but she felt so helpless, and she broke down and sobbed.

By December 2019, Sharron was just about strong enough to move back home and she could hobble about on crutches. A rota of friends stayed with her overnight to look after her and kind neighbours dropped meals off for her.

Sharron was living day-to-day but she told herself there would be light at the end of the tunnel. She knew what she had to do and she had to get through it.

She tried to think practically: it was going to take at least three months for her spine to heal and then she faced eight months of rehab. Her main goal was to get back to work. Sharron knew she needed to maintain a certain level of fitness to stay in the Navy and she would be devastated if she had to be medically discharged. The Navy was her life. She'd served in it for twenty-eight years, having decided that she wanted to be a naval nurse at the age of thirteen.

Sharron tried to stay positive but some days it was harder than others. She woke up one morning with her heart heavy in her chest. Her old life had been so active and busy, and now the days felt so endless that they all blurred into one another. Each and every day was the same: rehab, rest and constant pain, some restless sleep, and then it would start all over again.

She gave herself a pep talk.

You can do this Sharron, she told herself. *You can get through it.*

It was hard to keep going but she had to focus on her goals – she wanted to run again, she wanted to drive again and most of all she wanted to go back to work.

One weekend, Kay, a friend from the Navy, came to stay with Sharron while she was doing a course that was close to her house. They hadn't seen each other for a while but were friends on Facebook. Kay commented on the fact that Sharron's feed was full of photos of Taz and of her neighbours' dogs that she had walked.

'I saw something the other day and it made me think of you,' she told her.

Kay had spotted an advert in the British Forces magazine for a TV programme looking for people in the military who wanted to adopt a rescue a dog.

'You should do it,' she said. 'I think you need a dog back in your life Sharron.'

'I think maybe you're right,' she replied.

It planted the seed of an idea in Sharron's mind. When

Taz had first died she was adamant that she would never get another dog. But now, nearly seven months later, things had changed.

She would never forget Taz but she'd got over that intense grief and now she felt ready to get emotionally attached to another dog. In fact, after everything that she'd been through since her freak accident, she needed that. Sharron had missed the closeness and companionship that a dog brought. She missed having a wingman in her life. She knew both her heart and her head were ready.

In a way, it was the perfect time. Sharron was at home all day with months of rehab ahead of her. She still couldn't drive but she was out of the brace and walking without crutches now. She'd just completed a two-week spinal injuries course which had improved her strength and mobility and she had all the time in the world to devote to a dog.

In March 2019, Sharron was driven to Woodgreen by her mum, Wendy. She told pet advisor Lizzie how she was looking for a medium-sized dog, aged two to three years old who would encourage her to be active once her back had healed.

She mentioned that she loved Labradors so when they matched her with a black Labrador cross called Loki, Sharron couldn't have been more thrilled.

'He's had a bit of a troubled life,' Lizzie told her. 'He'd been living in a bedsit and his home life was noisy and chaotic.'

She was warned that Loki hadn't socialized with other

people or animals much, he was a little bit exuberant and he didn't get on with men. With Sharron's interest in training and the fact she was happily single, she wasn't particularly put off by either of those things.

As soon as his handler led him into the meeting pen, Sharron couldn't stop smiling. Loki was beautiful and he responded to her straight away – sitting on command and offering his paw in return for a treat.

'You're such a clever boy,' she grinned.

Sharron's mind was made up and she had no reservations whatsoever. She was going to take him.

However, it was only when she took him for a walk that the doubts started to creep in.

Loki was such a young, lovable boy, everything was so exciting for him and he had boundless energy. Sharron loved that about him but as she walked him around the grounds at Woodgreen, he suddenly pulled on the lead. Sharron lurched forward and she felt pain shoot up her back. Perhaps she'd been in denial but she knew then that Loki was too big, boisterous and powerful for her and she couldn't take him.

Devastated, she explained to Lizzie that she couldn't risk him injuring her.

'I loved meeting him but he's not a viable option for me,' she told her sadly. 'If I took him, I would be letting him down because I'm not physically strong enough to be able to manage him.'

It broke her heart but she couldn't risk it.

Sharron felt awful letting any dog down and she went back to the main building and cried.

'We don't ever want a good home to go to waste,' Lizzie reassured her. 'We will find you another dog.'

Back in the office, the answer was right in front of her, curled up in a dog bed. Bluebell was a six-week-old stray puppy who had been abandoned in a shop doorway. She was a lurcher-terrier cross and she had been too tiny to keep in kennels so a member of the Woodgreen staff was fostering her. Because she'd been taken from her mother far too early, she had separation issues and was very clingy and slept in her foster mum's bed.

Sharron wasn't expecting a puppy and as Lizzie carried out this tiny, whimpering creature, it was a complete surprise. As she gently held her in her arms, she felt her heart melt. Bluebell had just woken up from a nap and was all shivery and sleepy. She looked so bewildered and scared, Sharron's heart went out to her.

'It's all right sweetheart,' she whispered, desperately trying to comfort her. 'It's all right darling.'

She hadn't considered a puppy but it didn't put her off. She knew that she would enjoy training her and the timing was perfect as she had all the time in the world to do it.

As she cuddled Bluebell and stroked her tiny nose, Sharron started talking to her.

'I know a story where there was a beautiful young puppy that needed a forever home. And Bluebell, guess what? That forever home was with a crazy lady called Sharron!'

Unlike Loki, Sharron knew that she could manage tiny little Bluebell, who wasn't going to pull her very far.

Even though she was completely smitten, Sharron tried to think logically.

'She's absolutely beautiful but I'd like to discuss it with my mum on the journey home,' she told Lizzie.

Back in the car, she told Wendy all about Bluebell.

'It's a puppy and I wasn't expecting that so I need to be sensible and realistic and think about the pros and cons,' Sharron told her.

She didn't want to make the wrong decision.

Her mum laughed.

'Sharron I can tell you've already made your mind up,' she said. 'I know you're going to take her, aren't you?'

Sharron laughed too.

'Who am I kidding?' she smiled. 'Yes of course I am.'

There wasn't really anything to discuss. It was love at first sight and Bluebell was coming home with her.

As soon as she got back to the Midlands, Sharron rang Woodgreen to ask when she could come and collect her.

Sharron picked her up two weeks later. The first thing she did was change her name to Lola. To Sharron, she didn't look like a Bluebell. For some reason, the name didn't sit right with her. She was young so she was very adaptable and she didn't respond to her name yet anyway.

The staff at Woodgreen had asked Sharron if Lola was going to be allowed to go upstairs or sleep on the bed with her.

'Of course she is,' she'd laughed. 'She's going to go everywhere with me.'

As far as she was concerned, her house was Lola's house.

That first night, Lola curled up with Sharron in her bed. It was wonderful feeling this tiny furball snuggled in against the crook of her neck.

In the morning when Sharron woke up, there was a little face staring at her, and dark, beady eyes looking straight into hers.

'Morning sweetie,' Sharron said.

Lola wagged her tail and gave her a little lick on the nose and Sharron was in heaven. It was an indescribable feeling and she loved having somebody else to care for again.

She quickly realized that Lola wasn't a morning dog. She snuggled back under the duvet and obviously had no intention of getting up.

Over the next few weeks, Sharron was in a blissful puppy bubble. She didn't have to rush out to work so she enjoyed spending her time getting to know Lola.

Lola would follow Sharron everywhere. If she left the room, Lola would follow her, and it was nice to hear the pitter-patter of paws on the kitchen floor again.

When she watched TV, Lola would be next to her in her dog cradle. She was still amazed at how tiny she was, and Sharron had to carry her upstairs because she was too small to climb up them herself.

Her days were so different now she had Lola to think about. For the past few months, life for Sharron had become very dull. She had always been active but now she was trapped in the house all day, unable to go out much. It was all very mundane.

Since her fall, Sharron had spent a long time ruminating on it. What could she have done differently to avoid it? When would she be able to drive again and go back to work?

It wasn't healthy to keep obsessing like that and Lola gave her focus and purpose to move forward. She stopped thinking obsessively about her accident and dwelling on things, and she started to look forward to each day with Lola by her side.

One morning, Sharron woke up and already she felt daunted by the day ahead.

Every day she had a strict regime of exercises to do to help strengthen her core and back. But after six months of endless rehab, she was mentally and physically exhausted.

Each day was identical and relentless: wake up, deal with pain. Do some exercises, deal with pain. Do some chores, deal with pain.

She was a positive person but sometimes it all got on top

of her and today she just wanted her old life back. But then Sharron looked over at Lola curled up in bed next to her.

'I need to do it for you sweetie don't I?' she smiled.

Sharron knew that if she didn't get her pain under control then she wouldn't be able to take Lola for a walk. She felt a huge sense of responsibility towards this little creature.

She had so many things that she wanted to do with her in the future – long country walks, driving out into the countryside to go exploring, holidays in dog-friendly cottages – but she couldn't do any of it if her strength and mobility didn't improve.

So Sharron hauled herself out of bed, lay on the floor and got on with her exercises.

Halfway through, Lola came over to her, gave her a sniff and jumped on her.

'No it's not playtime darling,' she smiled.

It made her laugh and instantly lightened her mood. Having Lola around gave her the push she needed to get her through the final part of her rehab.

Lola also changed the way Sharron felt about being at home. Over the past few months, she had spent far more time at home than she was used to. After Taz had died, she'd wanted to sell her house and move, but now, because of Lola, her house felt like a home again. She loved seeing the box of dog toys and bowls in the kitchen and the dog bed in the living room.

She was never lonely or bored with Lola around. She chatted to her all day and Lola sat there and tilted her head as if she was really listening. Sharron had this little bundle of joy that was with her at all times and it felt amazing. She even enjoyed just sitting there and watching her because she was so entertaining.

One minute she would be running around at 100 miles per hour chasing her ball, the next she would be curled up in Sharron's lap asleep.

Sharron was determined to become more mobile again as she was looking forward to training Lola. She had done masses of reading and research into it and she had got it all planned out. Rather than just thinking about herself, dwelling on her injuries and worrying about the future, it felt good to engage her brain in something positive.

She loved to see Lola growing in confidence and developing her own personality. Like a typical puppy, she tested her boundaries, digging up the garden and tearing up bits of tissue that she'd stolen from the bin as well as a couple of pairs of shoes that were destroyed courtesy of teething.

Sharron knew she needed Lola to feel loved and secure before she could help get her over her separation anxiety.

The first time Sharron left her, it was only for a few minutes at a time. Over the next few weeks, she slowly increased it to fifteen minutes and then an hour. She'd put a gate on the stairs because she was worried Lola was too small to get up and down them.

She couldn't wait to get back to see her. When she walked into the house, Sharron was astounded to see Lola sat proudly at the top of the stairs having leapt over the stairgate.

'I thought I'd rescued a dog not a deer,' she smiled.

Every day Lola made her laugh and Sharron felt like she'd been given her spark back and made to feel more like her old self.

In August 2020, Sharron went back to work and Lola went to doggy daycare. Sharron loved her job, but she couldn't wait to get back home every evening and settle down on the sofa with Lola.

She even dipped her toe back into the dating scene and had a brief relationship. But it only lasted a few months and they ended it by mutual agreement. It made Sharron realize she was very happy to be single. The great love in her life was Lola and, besides her friends and family, she didn't need anyone else.

At weekends, they went exploring together. After a tiring week at work, Sharron loved going on long walks in the countryside with Lola. Lola loved all the new sights and smells and Sharron could feel her stresses and strains disappear as they discovered new places together.

When lockdown happened seven months later, Sharron was so happy to be back home with Lola all day. While she worked, Lola flopped on the sofa next to her and Sharron would take her out for a walk three times a day.

Sharron was working with her headset on one day when Lola sat down in front of her. She squeaked at her and her head pointed towards the front door.

'We can't go out for a walk just yet sweetie,' Sharron told her.

The next minute, Lola got a tennis ball in her mouth and threw it at Sharron.

'I think I'm getting the hint Lola,' she said.

When Lola got a toy in her mouth, sprung up and started squeaking it in Sharron's face, she knew it was time to come off her Skype call.

'OK darling,' she smiled. 'You win. Let's go out and play.'

Sharron still had to do daily exercises and lots of walking to help her back, and Lola was always a good reminder to get up, move around and go out.

She brought so much fun and joy to Sharron's life. They'd play chase in the garden together – sometimes Lola would chase Sharron and sometimes it was the other way round. Sharron thought her neighbours must think she was mad if they looked out and saw her.

Lots of her neighbours got dogs during lockdown and because they weren't able to take them to puppy classes, Sharron and Lola became their unofficial trainers.

Lola has also taught her a valuable lesson. Don't decide not to get a dog because you are scared of losing them. If Sharron had done that then she would have missed out on Lola.

Sharron will never forget Taz and she will always miss her. She had been her first dog, and she'll always have a special place in her heart. But Lola has brought joy back into her life again.

She has also inspired Sharron to have a change of career. When she leaves the Navy, she's going to become a full-time dog trainer. She has so enjoyed training Lola, and it has given Sharron the confidence to train other dogs. She has shown her that there is something else she's good at other than nursing. Because of Lola, she knows that that is going to be her life after the Navy.

Lola came into her life when she needed someone the most. She brought fun and hope and helped her get through those final months of rehab. Thanks to Lola, Sharron has her wingman back.

CHAPTER TWELVE

Pebbles

As David Hill's eyes flickered open, panic filled his chest. Groggy and in pain, he realized he was lying in a hospital bed and instinctively he knew that his career as an athlete was over.

This can't be happening, he told himself. *It can't be real.*

He had been born without a left hand or lower forearm, but his parents Gill and James had always instilled in him that there was no such word as 'can't'. Growing up near the sea in Devon, he'd learnt to swim by the time he was three, had started entering competitions when he was eight and was swimming internationally by the age of twelve.

In 2004, David had been Team GB's youngest Paralympian when he'd made the 100-metre backstroke finals in Athens.

After failing to qualify for the 2008 Paralympics by a frustrating 0.2 of a second, he'd switched his focus to London 2012.

He was twenty-three now and after the past eight years of training, David was in the best form of his life and at the pinnacle of his swimming career. Although he'd won numerous medals at European and World Championships, he'd never made the podium at the Paralympics. London 2012 was his big chance to win a medal and where better than on home turf?

His preparation had been going brilliantly – until he'd developed an excruciating pain in his lower abdomen. When he couldn't ignore it any longer, he'd gone to the GP surgery.

'It could possibly be appendicitis,' the doctor told him after an examination. 'You need to go straight to A&E to get it checked out.'

Instead, David had gone into complete denial. With just over a week to go before the Paralympic qualifiers, he couldn't believe that this was happening to him. There was no way he was going to let anything jeopardise his chance to compete in London 2012. So, on the way home from the doctor, he'd gone into the chemist and brought every type of medication that he could find.

Nothing worked and he ignored it for another three days until the pain had become completely unbearable. Now here he was, lying in a hospital bed, waking up from an emergency operation to remove his appendix, with the crushing realisation that his Paralympic dream was over and the last eight years of training had all been in vain.

The surgeon confirmed his worst fears.

'I'm afraid your high level of fitness meant the operation was particularly problematic,' he told him.

He explained that David had so little body fat on his torso that he'd had to cut through layers of muscle in order to even get to his appendix. There was so much scar tissue, his recovery time was going to be at least six weeks.

Six weeks.

They were the words David didn't want to hear; in fact, he refused to believe them. With the Paralympic qualifiers only days away, he was going to do everything he could to get back into the water.

He was back at the pool four days after the operation, determined to prove the surgeon wrong. Wincing in pain, he lowered his bandaged, battered body into the water. At the start of a 100-metre backstroke race, competitors have to do a specific type of dive that involves pushing off the wall with their feet and arching themselves backwards into the water.

David held his breath as his coach gave him the signal but as he tried to do his usual manoeuvre, red-hot pain ripped through his abdomen. As an athlete, he'd been taught to push through pain but, with a sinking realization, he knew that this time he couldn't. He couldn't physically arch his body to get into that starting position any more. With days to go before the trials, even though his mind was willing him to do it, his body was saying no. He needed to reach a certain time to qualify and there was no way he could make it. He was forced to accept his Paralympic dream really was finally over. Not only that, the scar tissue and muscle damage were so severe, he was never going to be able to swim competitively again. A few weeks later, a devastated David announced his retirement.

Six months later, it was the London 2012 Paralympics. David's parents had wanted him to go on holiday with them to Greece to help take his mind off things and stop him dwelling on what could have been. But he was so desperate to be part of it, he signed up as a volunteer. On the day of the 100-metre backstroke, the race he was supposed to have been competing in, he was volunteering at the rowing lake when his mobile rang. It was his mum calling to tell him that his beloved nan Mary had died after having a brain hemorrhage in her sleep. David was close to his nan and the two had shared a special bond. It was totally unexpected as she was fit and healthy – in fact, the previous day she'd been out shopping to buy her food for the week and plants for her garden.

David didn't know what to do. His parents were still abroad so there was no point going home. Alone and in shock, he found himself at the Aquatic Centre at Olympic Park watching the race that he was supposed to have been competing in.

As he stood there, high up in the stands, watching his friends and teammates, who he'd spent years training and competing with, getting ready to race, he felt numb. It was absolute mental torture and the only way David could cope was by shutting himself down.

From that moment on, he didn't know what to do or how to feel. He dealt with his huge sense of loss for his nan in the way he'd been taught to handle things as an athlete – he put it into a box and well and truly shut the lid. He couldn't grieve for her. He couldn't look at photos of her or talk about her, it was too painful.

Still reeling from her death and the loss of not only his Paralympic dream but also his swimming career, David felt lost. He was only twenty-three, but what was he going to do now? Being an athlete had been his life for so long. It wasn't a standard nine-to-five job, it was his whole sense of identity and without it he wasn't sure who he was any more. It had controlled everything, from the food he ate to what time he went to bed. He knew he didn't want to swim any more. He'd lost all motivation and being in the pool brought back too many traumatic memories.

David started working as an athlete mentor and did some work with young people facing disadvantage. He was supposed to be inspiring them but he didn't feel very inspirational. He was out of shape and starting to get aches and pains, so he started slowly getting back into exercise. He bought a bike and took part in his local Park Run every weekend. He also started swimming in the sea. He entered a local triathlon for fun and ended up winning it.

'If you put your mind to it and took it seriously, I think you could do really well in this,' one of the competitors told him.

His athlete's mindset kicked in once again along with that drive and determination to succeed. He started training more seriously and competed in several more triathlons. By the summer of 2015, David was a full-time athlete again. This time he had a different goal – to compete at the 2016 Paralympics in Rio but in the triathlon instead of swimming.

He moved to Loughborough to train at a specialist camp. But as he trained, negative thoughts came creeping back into his head.

The same thing is going to happen again. You're not going to make it to Rio.

As he pedalled on the bike, that awful feeling of waking up from his appendix operation replayed over and over again in his mind and he was terrified.

You're a failure. You've disappointed your family and let your coaches down.

He pedalled harder and faster, but he was convinced his worst fears were going to come true. Why was he putting himself through all this if the same thing was going to happen?

Mentally he was suffering but it was also affecting his physical performance too. He wasn't performing to his full potential, and after every gruelling training session, he struggled to recover. He was exhausted physically and mentally. He knew if he carried on like this he was going to burn out so, after a lot of soul-searching, he made a difficult decision.

He wrote an email to all his teammates confessing how he felt. He was embarrassed to show his vulnerability and his pride was hurt, but he felt he had no other option.

I'm sorry to let you all down but I'm really struggling. I need to take myself away for a few weeks so I can come back stronger.

It was summer 2015 and six months before qualification started for Rio. It wasn't ideal in terms of training but David knew if he wanted to make it to the Paralympics and perform his best, he had to do something drastic.

He hospitalized himself for six weeks and had talking therapy to help him deal with anxiety and depression. It helped but it wasn't a cure. David returned to training and several months later, he succeeded in qualifying for Rio. He wanted to prove to himself that he was good enough to be there and anything else was a bonus.

In September 2016, he finally made it to the Paralympics in Rio.

This had been his big dream and all that he'd ever worked for but as he walked around the Paralympic village, all he felt was tired. He'd finally made it but it had taken so much out of him to get here that he was struggling to enjoy it.

Competing in the triathlon took everything, every last

ounce of energy that he had. As he crawled across the finish line in eighth place, he didn't feel any joy. Just sheer and utter relief that it was finally over. A few weeks later, David retired from competitive sport for the second time.

Afterwards he experienced the same feelings of loss and emptiness that he'd felt after retiring from swimming. His relationship had recently ended and he realized that, away from competitive sport, there wasn't much else in his life.

He decided to start a business as a sports coach and motivational speaker. He channelled the same focus and drive that he'd put into his sporting career into his new role and soon he was booked for awards evenings, presentations, school visits and coaching. It became the norm for him to work 15-hour days and drive the length and breadth of the country.

One night David collapsed on the sofa, exhausted, after a long day. He knew he needed to try and switch off but as soon as he sat down, familiar thoughts raced through his head.

If he was sat doing nothing then he wasn't earning money or working hard enough, and therefore he wasn't a success.

He couldn't escape from the way of thinking that had been instilled in him since he was a child. In sport, it was that drive that he'd needed. If he was sat there resting, what were his competitors doing? They were out there training. The harder he worked, the more chance he had of success.

A few minutes later, he reached for his laptop again.

In David's view, his time to rest was when he turned off

the light at night and went to sleep. He had been conditioned this way for so long that he didn't know how to relax. Even though he was exhausted, he kept on working into the early hours. Work was also a distraction. If he was working then he wasn't thinking about the pain of 2012 or the grief of losing his nan.

Another day brought three engagements in different parts of the country. David hadn't been home in days and was living in hotels. By the time he'd got back to his room each night, he was too stressed to sleep. He'd lost his appetite so he wasn't eating properly, only grabbing quick snacks at service stations.

His appointment that afternoon was a speaking engagement at a school an hour's drive away. But as he gripped the steering wheel, David knew he was too exhausted to make it. He had to pull over in a layby for a nap so he could carry on the journey.

What have I done to myself? he thought as he sat in the car with his head slumped against the door, barely able to open his eyes.

His whole body ached, he hadn't seen his parents or had a day off for weeks and he was just so, so tired. He recognized the signs and he knew he was close to burning out again.

David knew he couldn't keep doing this to himself. He had to achieve some balance in his life. But he still couldn't shake that athlete's mentality that encouraged him to keep on going and told him he was stronger than he thought he was.

Harder, faster, stronger, better – these were the mottos that he'd lived his life by for the past fifteen years and the way his brain had been wired.

He spent the next week resting and recuperating until he felt better. But despite all of David's good intentions, he couldn't break the cycle and the same thing kept happening. He would work himself to the point of burnout for a couple of months and then crash and take a week off.

He only stopped when he was forced to. That happened in March 2020 when the coronavirus put the UK into lockdown. For the first time in his life, David couldn't work. All of his speaking engagements were cancelled and he couldn't coach at the pool or mentor people. The world had grounded him and he had no other option.

Overnight his security blanket had been ripped out from under him. Work had become his life. In theory, he should have panicked but, much to his surprise, he started to enjoy this enforced break.

In 2014 he'd bought a house in Devon. It needed a lot of work but he'd struggled to find the time to renovate it until now. He redecorated it throughout and put in new flooring and a kitchen and bathroom. He enjoyed making a home for himself and transforming the garden. Although David was enjoying not working as much, he was always busy and still hadn't learnt to truly switch off and relax. So, he decided to do something that he had wanted to do for a while and get a dog. His parents had a black Labrador called Dexter and he thought a dog would encourage him to get outside in the fresh air as well as helping him embrace a slower pace of life.

In August 2020, he started ringing around rescue centres. When he contacted Woodgreen and they told him about the filming, he was keen to be involved.

David had a definite picture in his mind of the kind of dog that he wanted. As he explained to dog-behaviour and training specialist Sue, he was looking for a small dog who was active, fit, outdoorsy and up for accompanying him on any adventure. She was quick to match him with an energetic Jack Russell called Ace who, on paper, seemed like the perfect fit.

David nervously waited in the meeting pen with his parents, excited to meet him. However, when Ace ran in, he seemed more interested in his squeaky ball than coming over to David. As he watched Ace manically tearing around after his ball, David suddenly realized that what he'd thought he wanted was completely wrong. Ace was the dog equivalent of him and that energetic side was exactly what he needed to let go of. He needed someone to slow him down and help bring out his softer side.

Sensing the same thing, Sue came back into the pen to say she also felt Ace wasn't the right dog for him. Instead, she suggested introducing him to a Shih Tzu-Lhasa apso cross named Pebbles who had only just come into Woodgreen the previous day. Pebbles had lived in a home with her mum and brother but recently she and her mother had started fighting so her owners decided they couldn't keep her any more. She was a little bit on the chunky side and needed to lose some weight.

As Sue led her into the pen, David's face lit up.

'She's super cuddly and affectionate,' she told him.

As Pebbles waddled over to him for a snuggle, he was immediately won over by her infectious smile and pink tongue that waggled around in every direction. She looked so happy and she instantly melted his heart.

Four weeks later, David finally brought her home to Exmouth.

He'd never owned a dog before and, at first, it was a steep learning curve. Pebbles explored her new home while he tried to work on his laptop. But his mind kept wandering.

Where was she? Had he made the garden safe enough or was there anything she could hurt herself on or fall off?

He couldn't concentrate on work or anything else because he was so focused on her.

As an athlete, he'd had to be selfish. Every decision he had made was about him and his performance and he'd spent his whole life thinking about himself. Even though it felt strange to have to think about someone else, David knew it was good for him.

He quickly realized that he was going to have to fit his life around Pebbles and not the other way around. She bonded with him instantly and from day one, she was like his shadow and followed him everywhere. She was extremely affectionate and just wanted to be cuddled and loved. She quickly learnt how to get David's attention.

He was about to do a work call one day, when she walked over to him and nudged his hand. He only has a right hand and she purposefully reached out her paw and pulled it towards her, desperate for some love and a stroke. And because he only had one hand, if David was stroking her then it meant he couldn't do anything else at the same time. He could see how much Pebbles enjoyed having his complete and undivided attention.

Even if he was engrossed in something else and couldn't give her attention at that particular moment, the thought was there in his mind. He'd do what he had to do quickly so he could make extra time for her.

Every day she came up with more inventive ways to get his attention. David was at his laptop one morning when Pebbles jumped up onto his lap. He watched in astonishment as she reached out her paw and closed the lid of his laptop. Then she stared intensely into his eyes as if to say: 'Look at me – I'm here! Why are you working and not spending time with me?'

It was quite overwhelming at first and he felt frustrated that she wasn't letting him get things done. But then he looked into her dark eyes and cute little face and it was the wake-up call that he needed.

What was more important? Going for a walk with Pebbles in the fresh air or sitting at his computer for hours doing a piece of work that he didn't really have to do right now?

So he pushed aside his feelings of guilt, went and got her lead and they spent a lovely two hours walking on the beach. He came back feeling refreshed and revived. That afternoon he sat down, with a tired Pebbles asleep at his feet, and did the work he was going to do earlier. He was far more productive and focused than he would have been if he had sat there staring at it all day.

Pebbles was forcing him to rethink and question everything. Why did he work? What did success mean to him?

For so long, he'd thought success was working every hour and making money. But David worked so he could have a lifestyle that he enjoyed but he hadn't had the time to do anything else because he was working so hard.

What Pebbles was making him realize was that he could still be successful in his work, but success wasn't sitting at his laptop and flogging himself for 15 hours a day. Instead, it was working for a couple of hours and then having time to walk Pebbles or go to the gym or see family. It was making a nice meal and then sitting with her in front of a film instead of working every night. It had taken having her in his life to make him realize that.

David's attachment to Pebbles was growing too and after eight weeks, they'd developed a strong bond. One evening, he was lying on the sofa when Pebbles jumped up next to him. She lay down on his chest, rested her little head on his heart and looked up at him. As she stared into David's eyes, something stirred deep inside him and he felt a huge rush of love. He'd only known this dog for a few months but now she'd totally stolen his heart. The strength of his feelings for her was overwhelming and he got quite tearful.

As he stroked her downy head and she stared up at him adoringly, it dawned on him that he'd never felt the same ever since his nan had died so suddenly. He'd become an expert at getting on with things and hiding his emotions and he'd never properly allowed himself to grieve. The hurt and the pain he'd felt when she'd died was devastating and he realized that since then he'd never truly allowed himself to love anyone again. That was his protection – if he didn't open himself up to anyone again then he couldn't get hurt and wouldn't have to go through that grief. But now Pebbles had unlocked his heart and was slowly teaching him to love again.

However, at the same time, it also made David feel very scared and vulnerable. With that intense love came the dawning realisation that he was probably going to outlive Pebbles. At some point, she was going to die and he was going to have to go through that hurt and heartache all over again.

Pebbles had unlocked his heart but she was also forcing him to face head-on everything that happened nine years ago that he'd buried. It wasn't just about grieving for his nan and learning to love again, it was also about grieving for his swimming career and the disappointment of failing to make London 2012. For David that moment he realized how much he loved Pebbles was a real awakening and he felt as if Pebbles was helping him to heal.

They started to develop their own routines and David particularly enjoyed the mornings. Instead of jumping out of bed like he had in the past, feeling like he had to get up and be active, they had a slow, leisurely start to the day.

To enforce some separation between them, David had trained Pebbles to sleep downstairs in her bed. Every morning, he loved opening the kitchen door because she was so excited to see him. She'd go outside to do her business then scamper upstairs to David's room where they had a snooze together or she cuddled up to him while he read.

He'd recently started to meditate as he found it helped his mental health and Pebbles liked to join in too. As he sat cross-legged on the floor, Pebbles sat in front of him. She closed her eyes and was remarkably quiet and still. He loved these gentle morning starts.

As the world began opening up again after the pandemic, there was the temptation for David to slip back into his old patterns. The work requests started to come in for speaking engagements and events.

Beforehand, he'd been willing to drive hundreds of miles and sacrifice a night's sleep. He had prided himself on being reliable and professional and didn't want to let people down. But now he had Pebbles, he realized he couldn't be out for hours and driving round the country.

'I'm sorry I can't do it,' he told people. 'I've got a dog and I can't leave her.'

He would never have turned down work in the past but Pebbles had given him a reason to say no and it felt really empowering. Now he had her, he realized that he didn't want to spend all day on the road and live in hotels.

His parents had also noticed a change in him since he'd got Pebbles. He was more relaxed and they saw a lot more of him. He'd meet them for walks with their dog Dexter and their relationship became closer. Pebbles expanded David's social life as well. He made a friend at the vet's with whom he went running and dog walking, and he also met other dog owners in his area.

She also transformed the way David saw exercise. For the first time in his life, he did things because he enjoyed them and not to compete or excel in them. He ran once a week or went mountain biking or kayaking. He joined a health club and even started swimming again as well as his daily dog walks with Pebbles.

Learning to genuinely relax was still a work in progress for him. Pebbles followed him around, waiting for him to sit down so she could jump on his lap. David knew that was where she was happiest so sometimes he would give in. He'd stop what he was doing and sit down and have a snuggle with her.

But there was still some internal resistance there. After a while, he'd get fidgety and he couldn't stop the thoughts running through his mind that he should get up and do something productive. Gradually, though, he managed to banish these feelings of guilt and learnt to enjoy this enforced downtime with Pebbles.

Some days he would get absolutely nothing done but they would turn out to be some of his happiest days.

David calls Pebbles his therapy dog. She's made him more emotional and more open about how he's feeling and has helped to bring out his vulnerable, softer side which he hadn't been able to express before. She's his reason and constant reminder not to overwork. She has taught him how to relax and enjoy the simpler, slower things in life. She has also helped him redefine success. Success for him now wasn't working 15-hour days or collapsing with exhaustion because he'd taken on too much. It was curling up in front of the TV with Pebbles or being able to say no to a piece of work or choosing to only work three days a week. She has helped him find his identity outside sport, heal his heart and bring some balance and peace into his life at last.

CHAPTER THIRTEEN

Poppy

Miles Pateman trekked up the hill, his heavy trolley laden down with parcels and mail.

'Good morning,' said a passing woman and Miles gave her a smile.

The sun was shining and he was outside in the fresh air. It wasn't a bad job being a postman; in fact, he was quite enjoying it. However, he knew it was only temporary because in a few short weeks, at the age of twenty-four, he was about to start his training to become a vicar and his life as he knew it was going to change for ever.

Both of Miles' parents were churchgoers at the local Church of England church and he was in the church choir before he could even read. When he was fourteen, he'd been at an event organised by his parish and the local Catholic church. They'd had a joint social after mass and the Catholic priest, Father John, had pointed a sausage roll at him and said: 'Miles I think you should be a priest.'

'Er? What? No!' he had spluttered, completely shocked and surprised.

However, it had sewn a seed in Miles' mind and when he was eighteen, he'd gone to see his parish priest, Reverend Sandra.

'Sandra I think Father John was right,' he'd told her. 'I want to be a priest.'

'Look, you're still so young,' she'd replied. 'Go to university and if the thought is still there then come back to me again when you've graduated.'

It was a little bit frustrating for him but he'd understood. Miles had also told his parents Alan and Kate what he was thinking.

'Well I didn't see that coming,' his dad had told him, looking very shocked.

'It's a big commitment but I'm really proud of you Miles,' his mum had replied.

They could see that he was serious about it and they were both very supportive.

Miles did a four-year German degree at Swansea University. In his final year, he had been walking along the sea front in Swansea when he'd had what could only be described as a calling. It was an overwhelming and all-consuming sense of God telling him that joining the clergy was what he had to do. Miles knew he couldn't ignore it any longer.

After he'd graduated, he went back to see Reverend Sandra and explained what had happened to him. Once again, he was told to go and have some more life experience. It was a huge decision to devote his life to the church and Miles appreciated that they wanted to be certain that he was sure. So, despite the fact that he was convinced that he would end up in the church, he had heeded their advice and was approaching two years working as a postman.

While he was working in the day, behind the scenes he was also having conversations with various people in the church who talked him through what joining the clergy involved.

Miles knew it was a very long and involved process. Even though he was sure it was the right direction for him, he was still nervous about it. It wasn't just a job, he would be devoting himself to the church, to a life of service and to helping people.

After working as a postman for two years, Miles handed in his notice. The next step on his journey was attending a three-day assessment where he faced interviews and group panels.

It was nerve wracking and Miles didn't sleep for several days. He knew the selection process was designed to help both him and the church decide if he was the right sort of person to cope with this kind of life. Thankfully he passed.

The first part of his training was academic and in 2015, Miles started at the College of the Resurrection in Mirfield, West Yorkshire. He was going to study for an undergraduate and a master's degree in theology in three years. He would also do several placements in different parishes and settings as part of his course.

Miles was an introvert and although there were others studying alongside him, he was much happier in his own company than hanging around in a big group.

He had so much academic work to do in such a short space of time that he spent a lot of time studying on his own in his room. It was intense, gruelling and lonely at times and Miles started to struggle with his mental health.

He was spending more and more time in his head, stuck in his own thoughts, and by his second year, he was approaching burnout. Even though he couldn't recognize it himself, Miles was sinking deeper and deeper into a dark depression.

The academic dean at his college came to see him one day.

'How are you doing Miles?' she asked him.

'Oh fine,' he replied. 'Busy and working hard.'

Just one look at him told her that he wasn't fine.

'Miles I can see that there's something seriously wrong,' she told him.

For Miles, it felt like a huge relief. He was the kind of person who bottled things up so it had taken someone noticing it for him to register that he was in such a dark place.

'I'm not coping very well,' he told her honestly and for the first time, he admitted to someone else how low he'd been feeling.

'You have to go to the doctor now or you're going to be in trouble,' the dean said firmly.

By that point, Miles recognized that he needed professional help.

The GP diagnosed him with depression and he started on medication and talking therapy. Slowly, it started to help and the therapy provided him with tools for the future to spot when his mental health was deteriorating.

For Miles, the academic side of college life was intense but the placements confirmed for him that being a vicar was something that he was committed to.

He did a parish placement in Lincolnshire, spent a month in Germany with a Lutheran church and had an amazing fortnight at sea with the Royal Navy's chaplaincy division. In the middle of his degree, he also had a placement with a hospice chaplaincy.

As Miles walked around the hospice, he was surprised. It felt nothing like a hospital and the sound of laughter and chatter rang out around the corridors.

He spent the next few weeks sitting with various patients and it was such rewarding work. He had assumed that he was there for the patients but it was his conversations with the staff that had the most impact.

He got chatting with one of the nurses in the corridor one day and Miles could see that she was exhausted.

'I'm struggling a bit,' she admitted. 'It's been an intense few days.'

The nursing staff spent so much time with these patients, caring for them and getting to know them and their families.

'You can't help but get close to them,' she told him. 'And we feel a huge sense of loss too when they die.'

They sat and chatted for about half an hour. The nurse did most of the talking and Miles listened.

'Thank you,' she told him. 'It's been lovely talking to you.'

Their chat hadn't been about religion but Miles could see how helpful it had been for her to have someone to talk to and offload. Each placement taught him something different about what it is to be a priest.

After he graduated from theological college, Miles got a job as a Deacon in Cambridgeshire. It was a bit like an apprenticeship – he worked in a parish but was supervised by a more senior member of the clergy. Finally, at the age of twenty-nine, he was ordained. As he stood there at the alter at Ely Cathedral in front of a congregation of five hundred people, Miles felt as if it was all a dream. He still half expected someone to tap him on the shoulder and tell him that it had all been a terrible mistake.

Miles was living in Cambridge and working as a curate in the surrounding villages. Every day was different and packed full. One day he had a church group followed by a school assembly, followed by a lunch and a meeting. Then finally he had to visit a family who had been bereaved to discuss the funeral.

As he got into his car and drove home, his body ached with tiredness while his brain mulled over a sermon that he hadn't yet had time to write. Miles loved helping people, listening and being there for them at some the hardest times in their life but it was also emotionally draining work.

He pulled up outside the vicarage where he was living. It was a newly built townhouse with five bedrooms on three floors. It was a ridiculously large place for one person and he rattled around it like a pea in a tin.

The whole place was in darkness and he felt a sadness as he pushed the front door open and fumbled for the light switch.

Miles loved his work but sometimes he wished that he could come to home to someone or something instead of a cold, dark empty house and silence.

Although his job involved him being around people a lot, there were times Miles felt incredibly lonely. Dating was tricky when you were a vicar and it was easier for him not to bother.

His friends were scattered around the country and the role of a vicar wasn't conducive to an active social life. It wasn't a nine-to-five job and if friends did come to stay it was at the weekend which was his busiest time. His only day off was a Monday when everyone else was at work.

One day Miles was at his boss's house. Reverend Alice lived in a vicarage with five dogs – three of them lurchers.

He liked spending time there as it reminded him of how nice it was to be around dogs.

Miles had grown up with dogs. When he was born, his parents already had two – a cute corgi-collie cross called Snoopy and Bonzo, a golden Labrador that they'd found abandoned as a puppy tied to the gatepost of a farm. After they'd died, Miles' constant companion had been a rescue dog called Alfie, a collie-whippet cross who'd been a high-speed ball of fluff.

Miles was an only child so the dogs had been almost like surrogate siblings to him.

Miles was always struck by how amazingly friendly Alice's lurchers were. It had been a difficult, draining day at work and he was still feeling stressed when one of the dogs came up to him. The next thing he knew, he felt her entire body weight pressed up to him as she leant against his leg.

'Hello girl,' said Miles, giving her a stroke.

'Oh you've had the lurcher lean,' said Alice. 'That's what they do when they're with someone they feel they can trust.'

Miles loved the soothing feeling of this large, elegant dog leaning heavily against him. She seemed to know exactly what he needed and it gave him a nice moment of comfort after a stressful day.

'You should get one,' Alice told him. 'Dogs are emotional intelligence on four legs.'

'I think you're exactly right,' Miles smiled.

In Miles' mind, it had always been part of his long-term plan to get a dog and, for the first time in years, he was settled in one place.

In March 2020, when Covid struck and the world went into lockdown, all of Miles' meetings, home visits and masses suddenly came to a halt.

Instead, his days were spent on Zoom, the phone or email reassuring scared parishioners.

He would try and go out for fresh air but there was only so far he could walk around the block on his own before he got bored and came home. Some days he didn't even manage to get out at all. It would get to the end of the day and Miles would realize that he was still sat at his computer screen.

That feeling of isolation started creeping back and he felt those familiar flickers of depression. It was then Miles knew it was definitely time to get a dog. Living in Cambridgeshire, most days he passed the large Woodgreen sign as he was driving around his parishes. So they were his first port of call.

Miles filled in an application form online and August 2020 he had an email from *The Dog House* offering to help with his search for a furry friend.

Miles jumped at the chance. In September, he headed to Woodgreen and told pet advisor Lizzie what he was looking for. He explained that he was looking for a friend to talk to and bring a little bit of silliness to his life.

'I think having a dog would be very good for my mental health, which is sometimes a problem for me,' he said.

His ideal breeds were a Staffy, a greyhound or a lurcher. Miles knew he didn't want something like a chihuahua, as being six feet six inches tall he knew he would look ridiculous walking down the street with a tiny dog.

Some friends and neighbours of his had Staffies and they were so friendly and loving. However, Lizzie was concerned that a Staffy would be too excitable for a parish dog who would be meeting lots of people. Miles needed someone calmer and they immediately came up with Poppy.

Poppy was a two-year-old lurcher cross who'd come into Woodgreen as a stray and was then rehomed. However, her new owner had recently had a baby and it had been all too much for Poppy. As a teenager in canine years, it was a testing time for both Poppy and her new family. Dogs going through this stage of life can often find it challenging to cope with new things like a noisy baby. Her new owners felt they didn't have the time or the patience that she needed so she'd been returned to Woodgreen.

When she'd come back into kennels, Poppy had shut down emotionally and she didn't want to engage with anyone. Gradually, she'd opened up and begun to trust people again.

But she was still a bit jumpy, and she became quite stressed in her kennel. To help build up her confidence again, she'd gone to a Woodgreen fosterer so she could live in a home environment and get some extra love and attention.

Poppy was still quite a nervous and shy dog but Lizzie thought she would be a perfect match for calm, gentle Father Miles.

Miles liked the sound of Poppy and he was eager to meet her.

'When you first meet her, she's a bit shy,' Lizzie warned him. 'It might take you time to bond with her but she will get playful and silly when she has that connection with you. You just need to make her feel safe.'

As Miles waited in the meeting pen, he was plagued by nerves.

What if she doesn't like me? he thought to himself.

When Poppy came running in, he immediately fell in love with this scruffy, hairy dog. She had such a lovely face and amazing brown eyes.

But Miles could see how nervous she was. As soon as her handler left the pen, she went up to the door and started whining and clawing at it.

'Poppy,' Miles said, desperate to encourage her to come over to him. 'What's this, girl?'

But she was insistent on staying by the door.

Miles' heart sank. It was obvious that she was scared and

didn't want to be there. He could see the relief on her face when her handler came back into the pen.

'She's still not sure about me,' Miles told her sadly.

But he refused to give up. He was determined to bring out Poppy's playful side and he picked up a ball and threw it to her. Balls were one of Poppy's favourite things and she couldn't resist tearing after it.

'Good girl,' smiled Miles, throwing it to her again.

Even though she was wary of him, he could tell she desperately wanted to play and be friendly, and he had a glimmer of hope.

'I know how you feel Poppy,' he told her.

It was almost like he was meeting the canine version of himself. Like Miles, Poppy took a while to warm up to people and preferred to stand back and observe at first.

Afterwards Miles took her for a walk with her handler. They'd been for stroll through the grounds at Woodgreen and they were stood chatting when Miles suddenly felt it.

Poppy, who was at his feet, suddenly pressed all her weight against him like a horse leaning against a post.

'Oh she's done the lurcher lean,' her handler smiled. 'When Lurchers want to feel safe they lean on a person they think they can trust.'

It felt just as comforting as Alice's lurcher and that small gesture meant so much to Miles. He'd been so worried that Poppy didn't like him and he knew it was a sign that she thought he was all right after all.

That was the moment Miles knew exactly what he was going to do.

'I'd love to take her,' he told the Woodgreen staff.

The paperwork was organized and a week later, he came to collect her.

'She's still very nervous around people she doesn't know so introducing her slowly and gently to strangers is the best thing,' Lizzie told him.

Miles took Poppy back to the vicarage and let her off her lead. She was very unsure and hesitant at first but slowly she started to sniff her way around. He wanted to give her the time and space to explore her new home.

It took her a few nights to settle and find a place that she wanted to sleep in. The first night, Miles put a bed downstairs. The second night she slept on his bed but she didn't like it and got a fright when he turned over in his sleep. By the third night she'd found her favourite spot on the sofa in the kitchen.

Over the next few weeks, they slowly got to know each other. Poppy gradually let her guard down, especially when she realized Miles was the source of all her food.

She was still very nervous of people and especially of men. Miles' parents came round to visit and his dad was talking when he gestured with his hand. As his hand came back down onto the arm of the sofa, Poppy suddenly dropped down onto the floor in a cower. Miles could see she was frozen with fear and very submissive as she flattened herself to the ground with her head lowered.

He wanted to reassure her but he made sure that he went over slowly and gently.

'It's OK,' he soothed, giving her a stroke. 'You're safe. We're not going to hurt you.'

He could feel her whole body trembling with fear and it was heartbreaking to see. The same thing happened a few times again. Poppy would cower on the floor when a man was making a gesture or a sudden motion with their hand. Sadly Miles realized that at some stage in the past she must have been beaten and sudden arm movements reminded her of that.

One of Miles' worries when he first got Poppy was that she would struggle to cope with meeting new people. As a reverend, the door to the vicarage was always open and his mobile number was public knowledge so people would call on him at all hours of the day.

However, a few weeks after he brought Poppy home, the country was plunged into lockdown again. In a way it gave Miles and Poppy quality bonding time as they were stuck in the house just the two of them.

Miles had found the first lockdown extremely isolating and difficult but this time it made a huge difference having Poppy there.

He was glued to his computer one day when he heard Poppy whining by the front door.

'What is it girl?' he asked her.

She always looked deep into his eyes and cocked her head like she was really listening to him.

He realized they were halfway through the day and he hadn't taken her for a walk yet.

Whatever was going on, Poppy forced him to leave the house twice a day so she could have a run round. Miles started looking into new places where he could take her for a walk. Walking through the local nature reserve with Poppy would boost his mood and clear his head. It really helped Miles switch off. He couldn't really be mulling over parish problems or emails while he was trying to keep Poppy under control on a long lead.

Poppy stopped him being trapped in his own thoughts.

She helped Miles appreciate simple pleasures like throwing a ball for her. The absolute joy Poppy got from chasing a ball was like nothing else that Miles had ever seen.

As long as he kept throwing it, she would keep going and he loved to watch her tearing around.

'Enough now Poppy,' he'd tell her but he couldn't face the pained expression on her face as she saw the ball go back into his pocket.

She brought some much-needed silliness and fun to his life, which Miles desperately needed especially during lockdown.

He was taking a call one day while watching Poppy out in the garden.

She was normally a very placid, laid-back dog but suddenly she was whizzing around the tiny garden at high speed, growling and barking at herself.

'Have you got the zoomies Poppy?' he laughed.

They only happened a couple of times a week but when they did, they really made Miles smile. Sometimes she would get them when he was taking her out on a walk and Poppy would spin around in circles on the lead.

Poppy had a favourite sofa in the kitchen that she had claimed as her own. She was lying on it one day and when Miles came back into the room, he burst out laughing at the way she was positioned.

She was lying on her back with her legs stuck straight up in the air as if she'd been shot. Her head was dangling off one side of the sofa with her ears flopping over her face. It looked deeply uncomfortable, but unbelievably Poppy was sound asleep. Miles laughed as he watched her twitch in her sleep.

Although Miles was always very gentle and affectionate with Poppy, she was yet to come over to him and show him affection. She'd done the lurcher lean a few times but Miles was always the one going over to her.

Poppy was out in the garden one afternoon while Miles was in the kitchen with the door open. He was sat down on Poppy's sofa reading, when she came trotting back into the kitchen. She took one look at him sitting in her spot, and she jumped up. Much to Miles' delight she flopped down across his lap and lowered her head so he could give her a love. It was only a little thing, but to Miles it was a sign that he and Poppy were really bonding and she was letting her guard down. It was the first time that she had come to him looking for affection.

In March 2021, Miles took on his first senior role in Port Talbot, South Wales. It was his first 'proper' job where he was in charge of a parish for the first time.

One of his main worries was how Poppy was going to cope with the move and he was concerned that she was going to be unsettled by the change. His parents looked after her while Miles organized the move into his new vicarage – a large detached house. By the time they brought her back a few days later, most of the unpacking had been done so all the familiar furniture and her things were there. Much to Miles' surprise, she settled in instantly.

Miles didn't know anyone in his new parish but he found that Poppy was a great icebreaker. They'd moved around the same time as their episode of *The Dog House* had aired. Miles was walking down the beach with Poppy one day, when a woman stopped them.

'Is that her?' she asked. 'Is that Poppy from the TV?'

'It certainly is,' smiled Miles.

The first time he led mass in his new church, one of the parishioners came up to him afterwards clutching a newspaper clipping. It was a photo of Poppy that had been used in publicity photos for the series.

'Is that Poppy?' she asked him and they had a nice chat.

Miles thought it was amusing that people were much more interested in the dog than in him. Poppy gave him and them something to talk about and wherever he went in his new parish, people would ask about her.

When the world started opening up again after months of lockdown, slowly Father Miles' work started up again. He could have meetings and visit parishioners' homes. After a long day, he looked forward to coming home to Poppy.

As he pulled up into the driveway, he knew that she would hear his car and come running. There was an inner door between the front door and the hall and as soon as he opened the front door, he saw Poppy sat there waiting for him.

The minute the inner door opened, he was welcomed with lots of kisses and a tail wag. Every time he came home, Poppy was always there without fail to greet him.

Miles loved the fact that this big house looked properly lived in with Poppy around. There was always a tumbleweed of dog hair floating around and her toys and balls scattered all over the floor. Wherever he lived, he knew Poppy would always help to make it a home.

He talked to her too. If he got the right tone of voice, she'd tilt her head to one side and look like she was actually listening to him and paying attention. Sometimes she would get bored and wander off but Miles didn't take it personally.

Now Miles can't imagine life without Poppy. He loves having someone by his side in the evenings and she's always there to welcome him home. He's got her to concentrate on so it keeps Miles out of his own head and helps with his mental health. Poppy has grown in confidence so much too. She'll happily meet people that she doesn't know and she's really come out of her shell. If Miles is sat on the bed, she will jump up next to him and curl up and she's become the most affectionate dog. She just needed that time and reassurance, and together, they've formed the perfect partnership.

ACKNOWLEDGEMENTS AND THANKS

This book would not have been possible without the help and assistance of all the staff and dogs at Woodgreen Pets Charity, together with the families and individuals who have generously shared their experiences. Grateful thanks to Heather Bishop for her sensitivity in helping to get these stories onto the page.

Huge thanks to the Five Mile Films production team and crew over all the series of *The Dog House*, each and every one of whom continue work so hard to bring these series to life.